# TOWARDS DECOLONISING THE UNIVERSITY

# Towards Decolonising the University

A Kaleidoscope for Empowered Action

*Decolonise University of Kent Collective*
*Eds. Dave S.P. Thomas and Suhraiya Jivraj*

Counterpress
Oxford

First published 2020
Counterpress, Oxford
http://counterpress.org.uk

ISBN: 978-1-910761-10-6 (paperback)


Cover art by Natalie Robinson.


Typeset in 10.7 on 13 pt Faustina


Global print and distribution by Ingram

# Preface

*Professor Toni Williams*
*University of Kent*

Introducing the pathbreaking collection, *The Empire Strikes Back*, Paul Gilroy declared that the publication of that book in 1982 presaged an end to 'marginalisation' of race in academic settings (CCCS 1982). Much has changed over the past 40 years. Many disciplines now generate critical literature about historical and contemporary relations of racialisation, empire and post-coloniality. There are far more staff with Black and other racially minoritised (BME) heritages in British universities of the 2020s than there were in the early 1980s and the number of university students from BME communities has grown exponentially since then. Universities today have access to audit and kitemark systems to signal commitments to policies intended to reduce the risk of inequalities, including racial inequalities and activists have compelled some universities not only to acknowledge but also to redress their accumulation of wealth through colonial exploitation and to revisit decisions about whose lives become venerated in portraits on the walls and statutes on streets. These important achievements would not have happened without the hard intellectual, cultural and political work that is required to ensure that decolonising and anti-racist institutional changes occur.

Despite these changes not even the most optimistic critical scholars of equalities would likely accept that race is no longer marginalised in academic settings and much remains to be done to fix racialised inequalities in HE. BME staff in UK universities overwhelmingly occupy lower paid and more precarious positions than white staff and judged by their degree results most universities continue to educate in ways that are more beneficial to white than BME students. Searing political critique of the wealth that some universities gained from Empire and its legacies is too often brushed aside. While sector reports suggest that contemporary HE leadership acknowledges the need to eradicate institutional racism in universities, the glacial rate of improvement indicates that feasible solutions have yet to be implemented.

In these times and this context *Decolonising the University: A Kaleidoscope for Empowered Action* offers an exciting and timely intervention that can help to close the gap between universities' aspirations to inclusivity and their attainment of full equalities for all BME students and staff. The book deploys a distinctive mix of testimony, comment, observation, and critique to produce a rich body of knowledge about the experiences of students of BAME heritage who live and learn in academic spaces that require decolonisation. *Decolonising the University* is a reminder 'the classroom remains the most radical space of possibility in the academy' (hooks 1994, p. 12); academic, administrative staff and university leadership teams should be immensely grateful to the collective that authored it and their academic staff collaborators for producing and sharing knowledge that benefits us all.

### References

Centre for Contemporary Cultural Studies. (2004). *The Empire Strikes Back: Race and Racism In 70's Britain*. Routledge.

hooks, b. (1994). *Teaching to Transgress: Education as the Practice of Freedom*. Routledge.

# Acknowledgements

It is very difficult to mention all the people whose efforts have made the compilation of this book possible. We would firstly like to acknowledge the contributions of those who have preceded us in this space and on this journey particularly women of colour such as bell hooks whose trilogy on feminist and critical race pedagogies (*Teaching to Transgress: Education as the Practice of Freedom* [1994]) has been a particular inspiration. Their efforts and contributions so often marginalised and excluded from the 'canon' have laid the foundation for us to do this work. We would also like to thank Dr Jason Arday for his inspiring words on survival and wellbeing in the academy in his keynote at the launch of the project on World Mental Health Day 2018, as well as his ongoing support and drive to share this body of work. Building the Anti-racist Classroom (BARC) Collective have also played an ongoing and special role in sticking with us and supporting the work of the project by patiently and so generously welcoming and facilitating our students at their events along with Decolonise QMUL and training staff at Kent and beyond. The quiet encouragement, affirmation and show of solidarity from activists-scholars, other student groups, academics and professional services staff across higher education nationally and internationally cannot be overstated. We owe a particular debt of gratitude to Professor Toni Williams for her enduring support and much more, to Professor April McMahon for providing initial funding and enthusiasm for the project and also thanks to our local branches of UCU and UNISON for their financial assistance. We also want to acknowledge other Kent colleagues including our *white allies* (you know yourselves), without whose support and advocacy, this journey would have been a bit more complicated. Our greatest acknowledgement is to the students, the change agents. Your passion and hunger for knowledge inspires us and provides the impetus for us to facilitate and continue to do intersectional anti-racism work, albeit within the 'diversity' agenda framework. This collective labour and solidarity is in search of social justice for all.

# Contents

# Introduction: The Dissonant State of Affairs in the Academy and the Audacity of a Kaleidoscope for Change

*Dave S.P. Thomas and Dr. Suhraiya Jivraj*
*University of Kent*

> Paradoxically, it is the act of resistance itself that is our triumph. These small and simple decisions to resist domination, added and multiplied can create significant momentum ... It is the refusal to remain silent in itself, that gives strength and empowerment in a society determined to cling to established habits of repression
>
> (Taylor 2016, p. 9)

The academic project is often presented as being incompatible with social justice imperatives that demands a redress of racial inequalities through vehicles of educational equity and decolonisation. The academic project arguably aims to remain an economically viable enterprise, operationalised through global competition and neoliberal consumerism. Social justice imperatives in higher education proposes a dismantling of false universalism that masquerades in the form of 'Westernised' or Eurocentric cannons that attributes truth only to Western scholars' knowledge and modes of knowledge production. This false universalism arguably endorses institutional racism that facilitates structural inequalities. It cannot be denied that racism remains an integral part of the lived experiences of people of colour in higher education globally. Set within the rapidly changing context of race, class, gender, sexuality and various intersectional relations on campuses across the globe, students and staff have been imagining and re-imagining the purposes and functioning of a university, in order to promote social justice and educational equity.

The process of students mobilising for social change in regards to their education is not a new one and also not geographically delimited. In fact, student movements in areas of the (post)colonised global south have generated a decolonising momentum that has been inspiring diasporas across the global north. One such example includes histories of colonial occupation (Portuguese colonialism) that have provided the grounds for what today are highly unequal higher education systems in Brazil. The results of the 2010 Census conducted by the Brazilian Institute of Geography and Statistics showed that the black population totalled 50.7% – 7.6% *preto* (those who self-identify as black) and 43.1% *pardo* (those who self-identify as brown). But talking about race and racism is generally avoided, even though it determines people's opportunities and life chances as a fundamental dimension of social life. Instead, inequality is attributed to social class and what transpires is in Bonilla-Silva's words, 'profound racism without racists' (2014). The struggle for equality in education systems in Brazil were present since the middle of the last century (Bernardino-Costa and Fernando 2013). The struggle was triggered by black students, a few professors and the black movement who demanded affirmative action in education (Nascimento 2003). On 20 November 1995, a march attended by about 30,000 in the capital Brasilia resulted in the delivery of the 'Overcoming Racism and Racial Inequality Program' by the President of the Republic. Central to the program's proposals was a proposition of affirmative action for black students in Brazilian universities (Moura and Jonatas 2002). The constitutionality of affirmative action was subsequently unanimously approved by the Supreme Court, guaranteeing access to students from public schools, poor students, black (*preto*), brown (*pardo*) and indigenous (*indigena*) students in the federal universities of Brazil, under federal law in 2012 (the so-called 'Quota Law').[1] In spite of this, affirmative action programmes across the country appeared heterogeneous as the decision divided opinion, with actors citing a 'violation of the principle of merit, ... reinforcement of prejudice against blacks, ...[administrative hindrances due to difficulty in defining] who is black or mixed race, ... and the absence of blacks in universities' (Bernardino-Costa and De Carli Blackman 2017, p. 377). However, to what extent did the anti-racist struggle in Brazilian universities end with the guarantee of access to black students on undergraduate courses? The court made affirmative action constitutional but did not mandate that universities adopt an affirmative action program. By way of interpretation, the *Quota Law* suggested that race was trumped by class, as indicated by its hierarchical position amongst its articles.[2] As in the landmark case *Brown v Board of Education*, the *Quota Law* in Brazil signalled a victory for proponents of race equality by way of affirmative action; but did it? Perhaps by way of 'false' liberty! The struggle for race equality continues in Brazilian universities.

> The decolonisation movement has become a home of hope for many seeking radical change in education. It has also, however, created unease among others, including students and faculty, as it has adopted a race-based rationale to press its demands. (Long 2008, p. 20)

Still, as a framework, decolonisation offers a kaleidoscope to illuminate the dissonant state of affairs in contemporary higher education globally in myriad ways. However, what did the student revolt in South Africa in late 2015 to mid 2016 mean to the amplification of student voices in higher education globally to effect sustainable change? How does this affect higher education and #MustFall, #Decolonise and #WhyIs movements globally? On 8 March 2015, the Rhodes Must Fall (RMF) Movement was ignited at the campus of the University of Cape Town (UCT), when student activist Chumani Maxwele threw human *faeces* on a statue of the British born imperialist, colonialist, politician and one of the key figures in the nineteenth century 'scramble for Africa' Cecil John Rhodes. Rhodes Must Fall can be situated in the landscape of social movements. Rhodes statue was a space of contestation prior to the excrement issue in 2015, when students believed that the statue served as a symbol of white supremacy. The students called for the removal of the Cecil Rhodes statue and an end to institutional racism in the university. The events that followed led to the removal of the statue of Rhodes from its pedestal, exactly a month after the '*faeces*' incident. The removal of the statue may have signalled 'false' liberty.

Subsequently, within a month following this incident at UCT, the Must Fall movement had spread to Europe as a sustained protest under the #RhodesMustFall banner at Oxford University in the United Kingdom since 2015. Oxford was one of the first locations outside South Africa where the questioning of the legacy of colonial expansion in the academe gained serious momentum. A statue of Cecil Rhodes was placed at the top of the façade of the main building of Oriel College, Oxford in 1932. The Rhodes Must Fall Oxford movement adopted a focus on academic culture, the impact of imperial past and curricula, in its call to decolonise the university. Its primary aims were: *1)* to instigate the removal of colonial iconography in Oxford, for example, scholarships (the Rhode's scholarship), plaques and buildings; 2) advocate for the increased representation of Black, Asian and minority ethnic (BAME) academic staff; 3) decolonising the curricula — presenting a broader representation of epistemologies; and 4) fighting institutional racism and discrimination at the university. Thus far, the removal of the statue of Cecil Rhodes by Rhodes Must Fall Oxford has been unsuccessful. Broader contestations continue.

In a milestone decision, on 17 May 1954, in what is immortalised as the landmark civil rights case *Brown v Board of Education of Topeka Kansas*, the United States Supreme Court ruled that separating children in public schools was unconstitutional (US Supreme Court 1954). Overruling the principle of 'separate but equal' precedent set forth in the 1896 *Plessy v Ferguson* case,[4] *Brown v Board of Education* signalled the end of legalised racial segregation in schools in the United States of America. The courts encouraged the decision by proclaiming that desegregation had to occur with 'all deliberate speed.' The promise of *Brown* had never been fully realised due to inaction. These marquee moments may have been etched in public memory. How does public memory contest, maintain or challenge inequality in the academy, particularly institutional racism?

Students in universities in the United States mobilised in solidarity in the form of gatherings and walkouts at many universities, including Princeton, Columbia, Berkley, Georgetown, Harvard Warrington and Michigan State. They argued that university administration were unresponsive to their concerns about racial discrimination, under-representation, racial harassment, prejudicial profiling of students by campus security and the local police, culturally insensitive Halloween costumes and other acts of inequality.

At Princeton university, students called for the removal of Woodrow Wilson's name from the School of Public and International Affairs. Led by members of the Black Justice League, which is an African American civil rights group, students sought to shed light on the existence of structural racism on campus. Students wanted the university to publicly acknowledge the racist legacy of Woodrow Wilson. Wilson, a descendant of confederate soldiers was the United States President from 1913 to 1921; he was postulated in some quarters to have practised anti-black politics and valorised the Ku Klux Klan, particularly in his book entitled 'A history of the American people' (Wilson 1902).

The shooting of 18–year-old African American Michael Brown in

Ferguson Missouri on 14 August 2014 by 'white' police officer Darren Wilson sparked several incidents of racism on the University of Missouri campus. Students and faculty subsequently protested. This ignited actions on other college campuses. For example, Yale University, Trinity College and Harvard Law School, where the campaign #RoyallMustFall was developed. Students demanded the removal of former slave-owner (who was allegedly brutally involved in the putting down of the slave rebellion in Antigua), Isaac Royall's family crest from the school's shield. Royall bequeathed 900 to 1,000 acres of land to Harvard college, which was later sold and the monies used to fund a professorship in law in 1815 (Royall House & Slave Quarters 2017). Harvard Law School educated former US President Barack Obama, as well as six Supreme Court judges. The shield's connection to the Royall family and slavery in particular came to light when Professor Coquillette shared the findings of his research that was published in 2015 (Coquillette and Kimball 2015). In protest, students had put the tape on mats displaying the Royall family seal to protest the inclusion of the family crest on the school's shield. A committee of Alumni, faculty, staff members and students debated over the removal of the shield and ultimately recommended its removal. On the morning of November 19, 2015, faculty members and students at Harvard's law school found that the portraits of some African-American faculty were defaced with black gaffer tape placed diagonally across their faces. This saw hundreds of students gathering for what was called a 'community meeting' in order to voice their displeasure. Addressing the gathering, a senior Administrator who has written extensively on topics like school desegregation, acknowledged that racism was an issue at Harvard Law School. In response, some students stated that 'the [school] administration had not done enough to make the school fully inclusive of minority students and faculty members and voiced an array of concerns that ranged from the relatively low number of black professors — there were twelve black permanent full-time faculty members out of 125 — to the way the school taught law' (Bridgood 2015).

Meanwhile, on 14 November 2015 the President of Georgetown University announced the renaming of four buildings on campus because their namesakes paid off campus debt in 1830 from the proceeds from the sale of Jesuit-owned slaves (Shaver 2015).

Days after a drunken white student hurled racist slurs at black students on the campus of University of Missouri, the statue of Thomas Jefferson, author of the Declaration of Independence and the third

President of the United States was covered with yellow sticky notes, calling Jefferson a 'racist', 'rapist' and 'slave owner' and more. Jefferson was a slave holder who fathered children with one of his slaves. There is a pronounced link between Jefferson and the university as professors can win a 'Thomas Jefferson Award' for excellence in teaching, writing, research and service to humankind; Jefferson's tombstone was also housed on one of the university's campuses. Students demanded the removal of Jefferson's statue, stating that venerating Thomas Jefferson validates rape, sexual violence and racism on campus. Students used the hashtag #postyourstateofmind and #Cognitivedissonance to share images of the post-it covered statue on social media.

Students at the University of Kent in the United Kingdom (UK) are now asking uncomfortable questions and have presented a manifesto to the university, audaciously proposing a kaleidoscope[5] for change. How did we get here?

Two years ago, we met in a café on the main campus of the University of Kent (UoK) to discuss rising concerns. These included: inequalities in academic attainment, variances in student experiences, increasing incidence of racial discrimination and racial violence on campus, the lack of opportunities for students to effect genuine change, identity and belonging and demographic representation in the curricula. We were mindful that there was a developing conversation around race, identity and belonging in the university (albeit slow) through an institutionally funded project that started in 2013,[6] a range of activities and initiatives by student societies (#UoKACS; #KentCaribbeanUnion; #KentUniISOC; etc), the Students' Union and the university as a whole, through its Internationalisation agenda, metrics, kite marks and corporate strategies. In spite of all these seemingly clear channels for students to articulate their concerns and opinions and for the university to receive these concerns and act with due diligence, we believe there was a lack of impetus. We grappled with the idea of amplifying the student voices, as agents of change. So tentative were we about operationalising our initial ideas that we decided to proceed with extreme caution. We were unsure how this idea would be received by the university, but knew that there had been an expressed need that was clearly articulated by the students through formal and informal mediums. This included Suhraiya's third-year 'Race, Religion and Law' module in Kent Law School, and student engagement with the 'Inspirational Speakers' events (including the hosting of the internationally renowned poet Lemn Sissay and MOBO Award winning rapper, intellectual and author of the *Sunday Times* bestseller 'Natives' — Akala [2019]), which Dave conceptualised as a holistic strategy to promote black intellectual capital as a pedagogy of hope in the academe (Thomas 2019). We also knew that we would receive support from the Law School, as this aligned with its critical law school ethos. Equally, we knew that we could gain funding through the university's Teaching Excellence Small Support grant (TESSA) and its faculty research seed funding. We had arrived at a consensus. We were going to amplify the students' voices and enable them to become change agents in order to develop a kaleidoscope for change. We agreed that this would be a process and experimentation of resistance within and against the ontological and epistemological traditions of the university (Jivraj 2020). We were mindful that 'speaking back' carries risks, as conversations about race-based inequalities are generally a 'no go' subject area. This is evident in the recent report by the Equality and Human Rights Commission 'Tackling Racial Harassment.'[7] While widely welcomed for illuminating universities' complacency in naming and tackling racism on campuses throughout the UK, the report was heavily criticised by academics and student leaders due to concerns about their lack of understanding of the lived experiences of racism in the academy experienced by students and staff from racially minoritised backgrounds. The report seemingly conflated prejudice by comparing anti-white British harassment with harassment suffered by BAME students and staff. Sarah Ahmed's (2009) detailing of the challenges in naming race-based injustice reminded us that

> the organisation becomes the subject of feeling, the one who must be protected is easily bruised or hurt. To speak of racism is to introduce bad feelings. It is to hurt not just the organisation, re-imagined as a subject with feelings, but also the subjects who identify with the organisation, the 'good white diversity' subjects, to whom we are supposed to be grateful'. (p. 46)

Speaking about discrimination, race and race-related issues within the UK higher education academy often lead to very interesting and uncomfortable exchanges. Some of these moments are generally to deal with power imbalances, the unveiling of the *Racial Contract* (Mills 2007), the proclamation of white ignorance (Diangelo 2018) and the silencing of non-dominant voices (Frankenberg 1993). Even in these contradictions, we have done this work, both participating in it and critiquing it from within. The success of this project lies in the unearthing of different formations of inequality in the academy, as we articulated in a response to the Universities UK (UUK) and National Union of Students (NUS) report #ClosingTheGap (Thomas and Jivraj 2019).

As part of the aim to amplify those otherwise silenced voices, particularly the range of experiences of students of colour in the academy, this collection is ground breaking in embodying what has been an ostensible and deliberate collaboration and co-production of knowledge between students and academics of colour. It was inspired by an institutionally funded research project in 2018–2019 'Decolonise the Curriculum', at a research-intensive university in the South East of England (University of Kent) and presents a Kaleidoscope for Decolonising a university. It operationalises conceptual thinking, fed into expressions of national and international student-led movements discussed above as well as others in the UK and elsewhere including: Why is my curriculum White?; Decolonise SOAS; Reclaim Harvard Law School (RHLS); #LeopoldMustFallQM; and Why isn't my professor Black? What they have in common is that they seek to unveil colonialism, racism, sexism, ageism and its intersectional inequalities with other (protected) characteristics, whilst also doing the structural labour towards the utopia of dismantling white supremacy in the academy.

> Given the prominence of decolonisation as a framework in student and teacher-led movements today, it is incumbent upon us to think more carefully about what this means — as both a theory, and a praxis. (Bhambra, Gebrial and Nişancıolu 2018)

As outlined in the methodology section of the Decolonise University of Kent manifesto (see chapter 1) critical race theory (CRT) (Ladson Billings and Tate 1995) and intersectional feminist scholarship (Crenshaw 1989; Mirza 1997) are amalgamated and proffered as an overarching theoretical framework that broadly undergirds this work and the project it presents. Through a range of perspectives and a multiplicity of diverse voices, in the spirit of counter-story telling, we reflect on the research project as a product and the process that has guided its delivery. Our reflections entail a diverse range of perspectives including race-based, gender, being LBTQIA+, religious faith and identity, culture, age and disability. Our reflections articulate how race and the varying intersections shapes the experiences of students of colour in the UK higher education in general.

The overall structure of the collection takes the form of twenty chapters, contained within eight sections; this is interspersed with a foreword by Professor Toni Williams, a conclusion by Dr Jason Arday and an Afterword by Professor Heidi Safia Mirza.

Section one contains the Decolonise University of Kent manifesto.

Section two presents the first of two chapters as exemplars of research students/associate lecturers operating in precarious conditions. This chapter by Anamika Misra explores the first of a series that is being developed on decolonising race talks around university campus landmarks and buildings. What does it mean to decolonise the actual physical monoliths of the university, beginning here with a college building named after renowned and influential economist John Maynard Keynes?

Section three contains short essays by leading academics in the field of race and education in the UK, who supported the project particularly through their participation in launching the manifesto in March 2019. They explore the potential for decolonising the university, the importance of student action in collaboration with academics of colour and recommendations towards realising sustainable, transformational change. First, the Building the Anti-racist Classroom (BARC) international collective of women of colour scholar-activists, presents zine-making as a framework for anti-racist learning. Then Dave S.P. Thomas writes in his essay reminding us where we still must go and what we still must be, in proclaiming that decolonising education requires a decolonial transformation, organised under the philosophies of social justice, in order to redress structural inequalities in the academe (Thomas 2020). Dr Barbara Adewumi then reflects on her experiences of doing diversity work with students in asserting that there is still much to do towards stripping the white walls of academia. Dr Joseph-Salisbury reminds us in his easy that in our efforts to decolonise the university, we need to look to history and remain radical, because the project of decolonisation and its threat to the white supremacist underpinnings of higher education. Dr Remi Joseph-Salisbury believes the project of decolonisation is at risk of being co-opted and presented as an illusion that this is merely a bourgeoisie concern of privileged students [that] fails to recognise precisely what is at stake. Professor Lez Henry then reflects on Inequitable Exclusion and Educability in his essay, then implores that the onus must be placed on institutions and faculty to effect positive, curricular change, because students' primary goal is to grow intellectually in an environment that is conducive to mutual learning.

Section four contains a chapter that presents the inspiring work of poet and author Suhaiymah Manzoor-Khan and the work she performed on 'British Values' at the launch event of the DecoloniseUKC manifesto. Her work — including Postcolonial Banter (Manzoor-Khan 2019) and A Fly Girl's Guide to University (Olufemi, Waithera Sebatindira and Manzoor-Khan 2019) — not only speaks directly to and reflects the students' voices in the DecoloniseUKC manifesto, it also unapologetically charts out moments of resistance and empowerment which themselves go onto do the work of inspiring others within and outside of the academy.

Section five contains two chapters. The first chapter explores the articulation of student voice through the digital mode of podcasts. It begins with a discussion by Dr Francesca Sobande (Lecturer in the School of Journalism, Media and Culture at Cardiff University) on the podcast series 'Stripping the White Walls'. She reflects on digitalised media as a key tool in amplification of complex experiences of students of colour within higher education and on podcast as a powerful tool for pedagogy. The second chapter in this section presents a reflection on the podcast series 'Stripping the White Walls' and 'Decolonising a Fool's Utopia' by Ahmed Memon and Joy Olugboyega.

Section six provides reflections of intersectional conversations with students as change agents. These conversations led mainly by undergraduate students through a series of twelve café style focus groups with seven distinct student groups. The themes include a discussion of the UK Government's 'Prevent Duty' and its impact on Muslim students on campus, outlining how different forms of racialisation affect them as bearers of both ostensible, gendered and less obvious markers of so-called religion. It also explores the experiences of young black men, international students and the theme of (dis)ability and racialisation as well as the process of a mix of students of colour from various disciplines and stages working together against being targeted by the shared label of being part of an 'attainment gap'. Herein also lies a chapter by the founder of the DecoloniseUKC research collective of postgraduate students, Ahmed Memon. He explores the questions and difficult paths involved in travelling the road to creating an ethics of decolonial research.

Section seven presents the strategic response by Dr Suhraiya Jivraj, lead academic for the project. This was designed in the light of the Decolonise University of Kent project that was delivered to the university. She highlights the struggle for institutional levers that may effect change and the costs it comes with weighed up against working with students within the neo-liberal university.

Section eight contains an abridged version of the poem 'Letter to the 1%' by rapper, activist and educator Lowkey, who like Suhaiymah Manzoor-Khan, Akala and others are key contemporary figures that are doing intellectual and social justice work relevant to young people of colour. This includes campaigning around issues like Justice for Grenfell and getting out the youth vote in the UK General Elections of 2017 and 2019 and tackling Islamophobia as part of wider (institutional) racism. This work is crucial for inspiring students through creative processes that enhance knowledge production and demonstrate accessible routes in for all.

The conclusion is by Dr Jason Arday, a leading figure in educational theory and social justice internationally. He draws together the entire project, tying up the theoretical and empirical strands from supporting BAME students' mental health — where his involvement in the project began — to the wider context of racial equality in education. He specifically highlights the implications of this project on the student experiences and the university's initiatives for 'student success' as well as the contribution of this body of work towards initiatives to decolonise higher education more broadly.

The perspectives presented in this book all share a common theme of decolonisation of the university. These are some of the reverberations that concern us. Our sincere hope is that it will inspire students to enact change no matter how small or large as part of their empowerment including holding their institutions to account to eliminate inequality and injustice in all formats. Moreover, this journey should be in collaboration with academics and others in higher education. After all, we are all part of and responsible for advancing social justice and equality of opportunities and outcomes for all.

**Notes**

1 LAW No. 12,711, OF AUGUST 29, 2012, available at: http://www.uff.br/?q=lei-no-12711-de-29-de-agosto-de-2012.

2 LAW No. 12,711, OF AUGUST 29, 2012.

3 Art. 1 The federal institutions of higher education linked to the Ministry of Education will reserve, in each selective contest for admission to the undergraduate courses, by course and shift, at least 50% (fifty percent) of their vacancies for students who have fully studied high school in public schools.

Single paragraph. When filling the vacancies mentioned in the caput of this article, 50% (fifty percent) should be reserved for students from families with an income equal to or less than 1.5 minimum wages (one and a half minimum wages) per capita.

Art. 2 (VETOED).

Art. 3 In each federal institution of higher education, the vacancies referred to in art. 1 of this Law will be filled, by course and shift, by self-declared blacks, browns and indigenous people, in a proportion at least equal to that of blacks, browns and indigenous people in the population of the Federation unit where the institution is installed, according to the last census of the Brazilian Institute of Geography and Statistics (IBGE).

Single paragraph. In the case of non-filling of the vacancies according to the criteria established in the caput of this article, those remaining must be completed by students who have completed high school in public schools.

Art. 4 The federal institutions of technical education of secondary level will reserve, in each selective contest for entry in each course, per shift, at least 50% (fifty percent) of their places for students who fully attended elementary school in public schools.

4  https://supreme.justia.com/cases/federal/us/163/537/.

5  The term Kaleidoscope is used here as a metaphor to capture the nuances of both the lived experiences and complexities of life on university campuses for students of colour. This was conceptualised by Lisa Shoko, Jasmyn Sargeant and Ahmed Memon.

6  https://www.kent.ac.uk/studentsuccess/index.html.

7  https://www.equalityhumanrights.com/sites/default/files/tackling-racial-harassment-universities-challenged.pdf.

8  https://www.theguardian.com/world/2019/oct/23/university-racism-study-criticised-including-anti-white-harassment.

## References

Ahmed, S. (2009). Embodying Diversity: Problems and Paradoxes for Black Feminists. *Race, Ethnicity & Education, Special Issue Black Feminisms and Postcolonial Paradigms: Researching Educational Inequalities* 12, pp. 41–52.

Akala (2018). *Natives: Race and Class in the Ruins of Empire.* London, United Kingdom: Two Roads Books.

Bernardino-Costa, J. and De Carli Blackman, A.E. (2017). Affirmative Action in Brazil and Building the Anti-racist University. *Race Ethnicity and Education* 20, pp. 372–384.

Bernardino-Costa, J. and Fernando, R. (2013). Appraising Affirmative Action in

Brazil. In: Gomez, T. and Premdas, R. eds. *Affirmative Action, Ethnicity and Conflict*. London and New York, pp. 183–203.

Bhambra, G., Gebrial, D. and Nişancıoğlu, K. eds. (2018). In: *Decolonising the University*. London: Pluto Press.

Bonilla-Silva, E. (2014). *Racism without Racists: Colour-Blind Racism and the Persistence of the Racial Inequalities in America*. Lanham: Rowman & Littlefield Publishers.

Bridgood, J. (2015). Tape Found Over Portraits of Black Harvard Professors. *The New York Times* [Online]. Available at: https://www.nytimes.com/2015/11/20/us/tape-found-over-portraits-of-black-harvard-professors.html.

Coquillette, D. and Kimball, B. (2015). *On the Battlefield of Merit: Harvard Law School, the First Century*. Cambridge MA: Harvard University Press.

Crenshaw, K. (1989). Demarginalizing the Intersection of Race and Sex: A Black Feminist Critique of Antidiscrimination Doctrine, Feminist Theory and Antiracist Politics. *University of Chicago Legal Forum* [Online]. Available at: https://chicagounbound.uchicago.edu/cgi/viewcontent.cgi?article=1052&context=uclf.

Diangelo, R. (2018). *White Fragility: Why Is It so Hard for White People to Talk about Racism*. London: Allen Lane an Imprint of Penguin Books.

Frankenberg, R. (1993). *White Women, Race Matters: The Social Construction of Whiteness*. Minesota: University of Minesota Press.

Ladson Billings, G. and Tate, W. (1995). Towards a Critical Race Theory in Education. *Teachers College Record* 1.

Long, W. (2008). Decolonising Higher Education: Postcolonial Theory and the Invisible Hand of Student Politics. *New Agenda* 69, pp. 20–26.

Manzoor-Khan, S. (2019). *Postcolonial Banter*. London: Verve Poetry Press.

Mills, C. (2007). White Ignorance. In: Sullivan, S. and Tuana, N. eds. *Race and Epistemologies of Ignorance Race and Epistemologies of Ignorance White Ignorance*. Albany, New York: SUNY Press, pp. 11–39.

Mirza, H.S. (1997). *Black British Feminism*. Mirza, H.S. ed. London: Routledge.

Moura, C. and Jonatas, B. (2002). *A Fundacao Cultural Palmares Na 111 Conferencia Mundial de Combate Ao Racismo, Discriminacao Racial, Xenofobia e Intolerancia Correlata*. Brasilia: Fudacao Cuktural Palmares.

Nascimento, A. do (2003). *Quilombo: Vida, Problemas e Aspiracoes Do Negro. 1948–1950*. Sao Paulo: Editora.

Olufemi, L., Waithera Sebatindira, Y. and Manzoor-Khan, S. (2019). *A Fly Girl's Guide to University*. London: Verve Poetry Press.

Royall House & Slave Quarters (2017). *The Royall Bequest and Harvard Law School* [Online]. Available at: http://www.royallhouse.org/the-royall-%0Abequest-and-harvard-law-school/.

Shaver, K. (2015). Georgetown University to Rename Two Buildings That Reflect Schools Ties to Slavery. *The Washington Post* [Online]. Available at: https://www.washingtonpost.com/local/georgetown-university-to-rename-two-buildings-that-reflect-schools-ties-to-slavery/2015/11/15/e36edd32-8bb7-11e5-acff-673ae92ddd2b_story.html.

Taylor, Edward (2016). Foundations of Critical Race Theory in Education: An Introduction. In: Taylor, E., Gillborn, D. and Ladson-Billings, G. eds. *Foundations of Critical Race Theory in Education*. 2nd Ed. New York and Oxon: Routledge.

Thomas, D. (2020). Belonging for 'Outsiders Within', A Critical Race Perspective on Whiteness as a Means of Promoting the 'Insider Without' Syndrome. *Encyclopedia of Teacher Education* [Online]: 1–5. Available at: https://link.springer.com/content/pdf/10.1007%2F978-981-13-1179-6_372-1.pdf.

Thomas, D. (2019). *Black Intellectual Capital: Towards a 'Pedagogy of Hope'* [Online]. Available at: https://www.advance-he.ac.uk/news-and-views/Black-Intellectual-Capital-Towards-a-pedagogy-of-hope.

Thomas, D. and Jivraj, S. (2019). From #ClosingtheGap to #ShiftingtheGaze: Tackling Institutional Barriers to Attainment. *Countercurrents: Critical Law at Kent* [Online]. Available at: https://blogs.kent.ac.uk/countercurrents/2019/05/16/from-closingthegap-to-shiftingthegaze-tackling-institutional-barriers-to-attainment/.

US Supreme Court (1954). *Brown v Board of Education of Topeka*, Shawnee County, Kansas, et al. [1954] US 347:483.

Wilson, W. (1902). *A History of the American People*. London: Harper and Brothers.

# §1
# A MANIFESTO FOR CHANGE

# MANIFESTO

*Authored by Wahida Ahmed, Hezhan Kader, Abdul Khan, Ahmed Memon, Joy Olugboyega, Anthony Otobo Martins, Mekke Orie, Jasmyn Sargeant and Lisa Shoko with Dr. Suhraiya Jivraj and in collaboration with Dave S.P. Thomas and Sheree Palmer. Artwork by Natalie Robinson.*

*Supported by University of Kent: TESSA | KLS@50 & SSP | KLS Centre for Sexuality Race & Gender Justice (SeRGJ) | Race Equality Champion |UNISON & UCU Kent | Student Success Project | Worldfest | Keynes@50*

## Summary

*Pedagogy and powerful learning experiences: The colour of our curriculum*

We need a diversity of perspectives, particularly from scholars of colour and from the global south (including access to *reading lists from around the world*), so that our curriculum reflects and addresses a range of experiences and *promotes cultural democracy*, as well as developing *all* students into critical and analytical thinkers and leaders within their education.

1. Race, identity & belonging: Promoting inclusion / countering exclusion

It is crucial to align Kent's Well Being & Student Support with the *diverse student population* to improve and encourage students to develop confidence and *tackle barriers in help-seeking behaviours* (such as 'circle of fear') and in turn *promote our belonging*.

This could be best achieved for example at the *Kaleidoscope Hub*: a principled community space where students of colour feel able to access and develop strong networks of support and *sense of belonging* and find help to deal with racialisation on campus.

2. Student voice & co-production with academics: Stakeholders within the university

There was also a lack of awareness of '*Black Scholarships*' including for students in stage 3 looking ahead to *convert Masters or PhD programmes* and that lack of full funding for students from the global south is a major obstacle. This is part of a blockage in the *career pipeline for students of colour* at the University of Kent. This has posed limitations on students of colour progressing to postgraduate studies and subsequently into academic positions.

A *Student Staff Forum* should be created, where the University has the opportunity to discuss, feedback and offer advice and guidance on issues particularly on *incidents of discrimination and unequal treatment* on campus.

**Methodology**

Students under the guidance of Dr Suhraiya Jivraj (Senior Lecturer in Law)[1] applied for Ethics Approval via Kent Law School and gained individual (online) consent from all participants in the focus groups to use the qualitative data from the sessions for this research. The focus group leaders (FGLs) were all University of Kent mainly UG Kent Law School students based on Canterbury campus. They facilitated the following 'café' sessions on Canterbury campus during February 2019:

• International Students of Colour (Jasmyn Sargeant)
• Challenging Ableism & Racialisation (Lisa Shoko)
• Muslim Women's focus group x 2 (Wahida Ahmed and Hezhan Kader)
• Muslim Men's focus group x 2 (Ahmed Memon and Abdul Khan)
• Black Men's group x 2 (Anthony Otobo-Martins and Mekke Orie)
• SSPSSR students (Lisa Shoko)
• Open to all students focus groups x 3 (Joy, Mekke, Jasmyn, Anthony, Lisa)

A sample of eighty students from across the University of Kent Canterbury campus (inclusive of all departments and stages of study) attended the focus groups, with additional individual interviews and input from students who stated that they did not feel comfortable or 'safe' attending the group sessions. FGLs opened each discussion with questions including on the 'BME attainment gap', student experience on campus, in and outside the classroom and in relation to academic and pastoral support.

Focus group leaders and the Decolonise the Curriculum Project organising committee (17 students) drafted the Manifesto in early March 2019. The manifesto is underpinned by values of *social justice and co-production* inspired by critical race theory (CRT)[2] and Decolonial Theory studied by a number of students within the project. LW623 Race, Religion and Law (convened by Dr Jivraj) and other critical studies (law) modules have been used as contextual frameworks and critical lenses within the 'kaleidoscope'.

The project has been led by the FGLs (as above) and facilitated by staff (Dr Suhraiya Jivraj [KLS], Sheree Palmer [KLS/SSP] and Dave S.P. Thomas [SSP]). It has also been by the KLS Centre for Sexuality, Race & Gender Justice (SeRGJ) as its first intersectional and collaborative student project under its new name (previously Centre for Law, Gender & Sexuality) where organisational meetings took place in its common room in Eliot College. The Manifesto is in solidarity with the 'Framework for Powerful Student'.

Experiences at the University of Kent: Final Report'[3] and responds to the Student Success Project Phase II research strategy.[4]

*Snowballing & Participation*

The focus groups were advertised throughout Kent Law School, departmental student support staff, Kent Union and student societies; for example, Kent Caribbean Union and the Islamic Society, as well as via word of mouth amongst peer groups. Some FGLs used Eventbrite as a sign-up method with a description on what the focus group would be about. These were advertised through *posters and social media platforms,* such as Instagram, Twitter, Facebook and Kent Union (BME network and welfare officer) and individual student WhatsApp groups.

Not all students who signed up attended and some students stated that they did not want to participate, as they felt it was unlikely that change would come about in response to the Project. Some even feared being under some kind of 'surveillance' from the university even though they were assured that their responses would be completely anonymised. Equally, some students did not want to be recorded. However, before the focus groups began, all participants were given information about the study, how their confidentiality would be protected and the right to withdraw. Participating students then gave written consent, including for data to be collected, through a recording device. *Trust in the focus group leaders and the Project emerged as a key issue to participation.*

Creating 'safe' café-style comfortable spaces was an important strategy employed to put participants at ease. This was critical, drawing on naturalistic methods, with open-ended questions ranging from social belonging at the university to academic support. This also allowed for spontaneous questions and discussion. The aim was to give participants a space where they felt comfortable to express their views and facilitate discussion around sometimes sensitive and difficult topics relating to race and racialisation in everyday life experiences, including hurdles in practising faith on campus. It was critical to allow participants freedom to safely express their ideas rather than simply interviewing them to draw out preconceived notions or expectations.

Location and refreshments helped to create an 'atmosphere' that encouraged free conversation for students to voice their opinions and concerns. Part of these factors was to create an atmosphere of relatability and shared concern. For example, the first location of the first group discussion on Muslim male experiences was in the local mosque on Giles Lane where some Muslim students currently have their own sense of community. This approach of relating to the FGLs on a level of shared identity i.e. common faith, experiences and association with the mosque, received a positive response. This was clear also when students were asked if they would speak to anyone else approaching them to share their experiences, they replied, 'no, we would not have even agreed to meet or speak to someone we did not personally know'.

Similarly, the general consensus amongst a lot of the female Muslim student participants was that they feel alienated, feel 'targeted', feel a responsibility to be representatives for all Muslim women, and feel that little has been done to make them feel that they belong in this institution. The 'Challenging Ableism and Racialisation' and the SSPSSR Focus Groups[5] were both held in the Centre SeRGJ common room. In order to make the participants feel more at ease, we provided them with pizza and beverages which created a more conversational atmosphere, conducive for the sensitive topics that we wanted to discuss, for example the challenges of being a racialised student battling mental health. The students expressed that coming from a non-white background, they sometimes felt isolated because in some cultures, mental health is viewed as a weakness rather than an affliction or illness. The seating was arranged in a quasi-circle such that everyone was able to see each other, contributing to a natural and conversational environment.

*Fluid Terminology*

Data from the focus group's highlighted that there was no one preference for the terminology to refer to the participants and their experiences. We therefore use BAME/BME (Black, Asian and Minority Ethnic); people/ students of colour and minoritised people, interchangeably below. The underlying and key point is to highlight barriers to learning due to racialisation[6] whether explicit, implicit, embedded, individual, institutional or otherwise.

**Project Findings and Recommendations**

*1. Pedagogy and Powerful Learning Experiences: The Colour of Our Curriculum*

*Phase II of the SSP (EDI) Project research points to the* "White Curriculum' as a barrier to inclusivity that fails to legitimise contributions to knowledge from people of colour.'[7]

• We need a diversity of perspectives, particularly from *scholars of colour* and from the global south (including access to *reading lists from around the world*), so that our curriculum reflects and addresses a range of experiences and *promotes cultural democracy,*[8] as well as developing *ALL* students into critical and analytical thinkers and leaders within their education.
• One way this can be initially operationalised is through *Reading Lists* centred on an understanding on *who* the reading list is for and *how* it is created. It is important to know what the purpose of the reading list is, and to ensure that there is an impetus on teachers to develop cultural competence and knowledge of a range of perspectives.

This is crucial to combat a narrow focus privileging the 'white canon' and perpetuating academics' fear of utilising other sources. We can promote academic 'risk-taking' i.e. encouraging students to depart from this narrow perspective and content. This can also be supported as part of the academic curriculum, for example though discussion outside the lecture/seminar space in areas such as the suggested Hub space (see below). These discussions could be student-led as with the KLS Decolonising the Curriculum Project discussion groups, including master-classes with leading academics such as Gurminder Bhambra.

> The only time we look at non-white material is in relation to colonialism (slavery/anti-slavery) or extremism and the material tends to be negative as opposed to positive. (Focus group participant)

> We are not trying to erase history or knowledge but enrich it. (Final year law student)

> It was literally white male theorists all the time and it was just boring because you cannot relate to it ... it was just not relatable. (Law student-focus group participant)

The notion of a *one-size-fits-all student experience is outmoded*. Students report that they attend university with the hope of *achieving personal growth* but that the opportunities for enhancement including employability and so on, that are on offer can often feel daunting and unsuitable especially when students are struggling to keep up with study and other commitments.[9]

> I do not want to speak up in class because I do not want to be that one brown kid who talks. It feels like seminar leaders and lecturers are more social with students that look like them. (Focus group participant)

Lecturers should be more explicit about what is expected from students and *'how to succeed'* during obligatory sessions e.g. in *Induction Weeks*. These sessions could tackle university myths and *set up high expectations* with sufficient time slots allocated for current and past students of colour and other professionals in the field to talk about what has helped them on their journey of achievement in a variety of formats (e.g. masterclasses, podcasts and discussion forums).

> When I speak, I feel like people are expecting a certain response. Everyone looks at me because of my hijab and have expectations. I often don't speak because I don't want to give people that satisfaction. I don't want to talk because you're not going to listen to (what) I have to say, you're just going to see what I have on my head. Besides, whatever I have to say, they're going to think is biased. (Focus group participant)

This is necessary to enable students to *see themselves reflected amongst (soon to be) graduates and to aim high*. It is also an important opportunity embedded into the curriculum for students to develop *trusting relationships* with academics and other students from all cultures and backgrounds.

### 2. Race, Identity & Belonging: Promoting Inclusion/Countering Exclusion

Phase II of the SSP (EDI) Project research quotes the University of Kent's Educational Strategy stating,

> we will ensure that *our staff body remains diverse*, so that our curriculum reflects and addresses a range of perspectives. How can this be operationalised?'[10]

In addition, it also states:

survey findings indicated that BME students were less engaged in campus life, yet the popularity of the University's African-Caribbean and Islamic Societies suggests that at least *some* students on campus have found a sense of identity and belonging on campus.

And asks:

Does Kent's range of student societies provide sufficient coverage for BME students on campus, or do certain populations feel socially excluded?

The *Kaleidoscope Hub* should be a principled community space where students of colour feel able to access and develop strong networks of support and *sense of belonging* and find help to deal with racialisation on campus.

The Hub could run sessions specifically for LGBTQ+ students of colour and non-alcohol and halal/kosher (freshers' week) events for those who do not feel comfortable within mainstream 'white' spaces. This could be publicised across campuses and promote *strong networks of support* especially for those wishing to access space and activities other than Kent Union or bars/pubs.

My whole time at this university, I have been alienated. (Focus group participant)

You're not welcome in societies if you don't drink [in initiations, for example].

It is crucial to align Kent's Well Being & Student Support with the *diverse student population* to improve and encourage students to develop confidence and *tackle barriers in help-seeking behaviours* (such as 'circle of fear') and in turn *promote our belonging.*

I don't use student support because there isn't anyone who can fully understand me or my situation (Focus group participant)

This could be best achieved for example at the Hub which would also be a centre for the *Kaleidoscope Network* including a community of voices facilitating collaborative efforts and setting up different schemes of mentoring including:

a) Staff to Student

• List of BME members of staff that are accessible to students.

• BME counsellors, mentors and health advisers (or trained in BME issues) even if only available for specific slots on campus.

• Student support through discussions on literature produced by staff of colour/from the global south and a list of 'critical race' learning/modules e.g. Race, Religion & Law available as additional options and publicised.
• Networks of BME staff should be utilised to support student development that would also link to (compulsory) academic classes on modules and encourage academic 'risk taking' (see above, to diversify the curriculum.

> They (staff) don't know where we are coming from — so I don't think that I can talk to them (Focus group participant)

b) Student to Staff

• Training new members of the Hub to be researchers and to collect data on student experience which is remunerated (as with this project).

> I want to see more staff that look like us and for us to know who they are. (Focus group participant)

• This would also facilitate students of colour to work collaboratively and become peer facilitators and change actors, develop employability skills and become leaders.

> I don't think I am comfortable talking to a staff who is not from my faith about any concerns I have when class timings or exams can clash with me practicing my faith. (Focus group participants)

c) Student to Student

• e.g. black and minoritised societies, reading/study groups aimed at, and specifically for, students of colour, student-led discussions on reading lists and teaching material.

d) Staff to Staff

• Need for more academic and professional service staff of colour on campus.
• Increase visibility in library collections with access to journals, research work not currently subscribed to by the library.[11]

• Set up a race/racialised religion equality network to support staff.
• Develop a *Kent-specific Cultural Competence Workshop* led by Kent academic staff (Centre for Sexuality, Race, Gender Justice) in collaboration with the Runnymede Trust (Race Equality Think Tank) and diversity practitioners of colour including students and staff. This could be developed for both staff and students.
• Any staff enforcing the Prevent duty should undergo Islamophobia training to develop cultural competence in order to tackle racial profiling/biases and understand the impact of Prevent as a form of racialisation towards Muslim students in particular.[12]

> In order to fit in, I felt like I had to compromise my beliefs. I had to change the way I dress, the way I speak, even what I say. (Focus group participant)

*3. Student Voice & Co-Production With Academics: Stakeholders Within the University*[13]

• Participants reported that there was a severe *under-representation of black academics or BME success* on campus (outside of the Inspirational Speakers Scheme) and seeing 'yourself represented' did make a big difference to engagement in academic life.
• There was also a lack of awareness of *'Black Scholarships'* including for students in stage 3 looking ahead to *convert Masters or PhD programmes* and that lack of full funding for students from the global south is a major obstacle. This is part of a blockage in the *career pipeline for students of colour* at the University of Kent. This has posed limitations on students of colour progressing to postgraduate studies and subsequently into academic positions. The provision of a number of *postgraduate scholarships specifically for students of colour* (similar to the Vice Chancellor's fiftieth Anniversary Scholarships) would be a proactive way to increase the number of students of colour transitioning to postgraduate studies and subsequently into a career in academia.
• Most participants (outside of KLS) were unaware of the role of Student Success officers and their remits on how to help BME students.

> Everyone needs a Shere (Student Success Project Manager in the Kent Law School), so why doesn't everyone know and get support from people like Sheree. (Back male law student)

It was widely felt that there was a dire lack of student consultation on BME issues and if this was happening via KU this was insufficient and other student-led channels should be created with a senior member of staff acting as a race champion or via a student-staff forum.

• A *Student Staff Forum*[14] should be created, where the University has the opportunity to discuss, feedback and offer advice and guidance on issues such as:
• Assessment patterns, including presentations
• Acknowledgement of controversial incidents on campus
• Developing a Students of Colour Guide to Succeeding and finding culturally accessible support.
• Equal Treatment by staff, particularly campus security for implementing policies by undergoing cultural competence training (see above). This could combat any student perception that they may be acting as an 'arm of the police in their behaviours and practice.'

> Student being escorted out of the building in case he 'got aggressive'. He hadn't done anything other than ask staff a question and it felt like he was being targeted or having assumptions made about him because of how he looked. (Focus group participant)

• Consulting on welfare/conduct issues particularly in relation to Inclusive Learning Plans (ILPs) and discipline which are perceived as unhelpful in obtaining support from teachers.

> ILPs are not looked at by staff so we constantly have to re-explain ourselves or be forced into silence as its easier that way. (Focus group participant)

• Training staff to identify and deal with discrimination in the classroom, e.g. Racism/Islamophobia and in relation to International Students.

> The student body on campus is diversifying exponentially, currently at around 38% and rising, so we are stakeholders of this university, yet we do not feel as though our voices are being heard sufficiently by the people who can effect change. (Final year law student)

• *The Student Staff Forum* supported by the Executive Group's Race (and Intersectionality) Champion would provide a direct channel of communication as not all students want to be represented or feel adequately included by the student union.

> In recognising that the University is a community, we need the leaders of the community (senior management) to be held accountable. (Focus group participant)

• The forum would also further indicate *institutional responsibility*, accountability and transparency as well as bridge (communication) gaps between students and senior leadership particularly about racism on campus.

> The University is a community and so it needs to act for the voices that are not adequately heard. Students are not interested in tokenism but being full citizens at the University. (Focus group participant)

www.decoloniseUKC.org

Decolonise University of Kent Collective

**Notes**

1 Deputy Director of Education (Decolonising the Curriculum) and Co-Director Centre for Sexuality, Race and Gender Justice (SeRGJ).

2 Ladson-Billings (2010) Just What Is Critical Race Theory and What's it Doing in a Nice Field Like Education? *International Journal of Qualitative Studies in Education*, 11 (1) 7–24, DOI: 10.1080/095183998236863.

3 https://www.kent.ac.uk/cshe/kentlogin/A%20Framework%20for%20 Powerful%20Student%20Learning%20Experiences%20final%20250119.pdf.

4 https://www.kent.ac.uk/studentsuccess/poster%20presentations/ Festival%20of%20Projects_2018%20-%20SSP%20research%20FINAL.pdf.

5 This focus group was added as an extra session to the original programme due to demand from SSPSR students who had attended the open ones but felt they needed a subject/department specific session.

6 'Instances where social relations between people have been structured by the signification of human biological characteristics in such a way as to define and construct differentiated social collectivities. The concept therefore refers to a process of categorisation, a representational process of defining an Other (usually, but not exclusively) somatically' (Miles, 'Racism' 1989, p. 75).

7 https://www.kent.ac.uk/studentsuccess/poster%20presentations/ Festival%20of%20Projects_2018%20-%20SSP%20research%20FINAL.pdf.

8 'Cultural democracy recognizes the human right of each ethnic / cultural group in a culturally diverse society to have equal access to life chances and sources of social power. Power means to have a "voice," that is, to have the capacity to define oneself as an active participant in the world rather than a passive victim' (Delores P. Aldridge [2000]. On Race and Culture: Beyond Afrocentrism, Eurocentrism to Cultural Democracy, *Sociological Focus* 33[1], 95–107).

9 According to the UKC report outlining 'A Framework for Powerful Student Experiences' (Quinlan 2019).

*i.)* Staff reported that they are frustrated with providing opportunities for enrichment and support that students do not take up. They believe some students are hard to engage. It would be interesting to find out to what extent are actually communicating effectively with students. Is the communication tailored to the student or is it a one size fit all model?

*ii)* What do students want from their learning experiences at Kent? Students (20%) reported that they wanted to enjoy what they are learning.

*iii)* How do hopes vary by background? BME students — more so than white students — reported that they wanted application-oriented? This means they want to learn things that they can apply to real world contexts, i.e. to achieve a job etc. Does the narrow perspective support this notion? BME students further reported that their hopes for university are not being fulfilled.

*iv)* Students also reported that their most powerful learning experiences involved learning and thinking and those aligned with the achievement of their goals.

10 The rates of BME staff on campus as compared to white staff is very low i.e. 9% BME professors as compared to 76% white professors (See Kent EDI Report 2016 page 48 for further breakdowns). This is particularly shocking given the increasingly diverse student body for whom it is important to see themselves and their experiences reflected at different levels in the university. See also barriers in relation to promotion, race pay gap etc. here: https://www.theguardian.com/education/2019/feb/04/black-female-professors-report; https://www.theguardian.com/education/2019/feb/05/talented-women-of-colour-are-blocked-why-are-there-so-few-black-female-professors; https://www.theguardian.com/education/2018/nov/23/universities-must-tackle-the-big-ethnicity-pay-gap.

11 This work has already started by PGRs in the KLS Decolonising Research Collective.

12 See the NUS guidance to Student Union Officers on the Prevent strategy here: https://www.nusconnect.org.uk/articles/students-not-suspects-building-your-campaign-against-prevent.

13 According to the Kent EDI Report 2016/17 'the student BME population has increased year on year since 2011–12 to 24.58%. Among the UK-domiciled student population at Kent, 12.69% identified as Black, much higher than the ECU national benchmark of 6.70% (Chart 30).

Students who identified as Black represented 36.29% of the K-domiciled BME population' (Chart 31 on page 55). It also states: 'At Kent, BME students comprised 25.68% of undergraduate students and 18.93% of postgraduate students.' Although focus groups for this project were not held at Medway there is clearly a need to conduct research there as there is a significantly higher BME student population at the Medway campus (36.84%) than the Canterbury campus (21.93%) and these figures are from 2016 it is likely to be higher now.

14 https://www.theguardian.com/education/2019/jan/08/universities-must-listen-more-closely-to-their-bame-staff-and-students.

§2

# AN EMPOWERED VOICE

2

# Decolonising Keynes: Between Memory and History

*Anamika Misra*
*University of Kent*


Faced with a collective forgetting, we must fight to remember.

(Reni Eddo Lodge 2018)


Recently, the University of Kent, celebrated fifty years of Keynes College. This commemoration celebrated the achievements and activities of the College, the academic schools it houses, and the wider university itself. The celebration lasted over the Autumn Term, showcasing a variety of exhibits on peace, immigration, and sustainability. Conspicuously absent in the celebration, but still present by virtue of the location of these celebrations, was its namesake's legacy. Like a Schrödinger's cat's version of history.

The third college to be opened at the University in 1968, Keynes College is named after the influential economist John Maynard Keynes — often referred to as the 'Father of Macroeconomics.' Best known for his contributions to economics in the form of 'Keynesian' economics, the canon of Keynes, as we know it, is one that sustains an image which is positive and even revered. Yet, that changed with a recent article by Patnaik (2018) that detailed Keynes' central role in the Bengal famine of 1943.

Coincidentally, the same year that marked the fiftieth anniversary of Keynes College also marked 75 years since the death of more than 3 million people as a result of Keynes' policies to help fund the cost of war spending by Britain and the Allied powers. The policy of 'profit inflation' (PI), defined by the deliberate rapid increase of out-put prices in comparison to wages in order to redistribute the income of the working population towards those of capitalists and companies (Patnaik 2017, p. 200), being the principle policy that led to the said outcome. Now, PI was heavily criticised and resisted by trade unions in Britain for being regressive and was abandoned in favour of taxation. But India, like all the other colonies of the Raj was viewed as a vast social lab where economic and juridical changes could be implemented with minimum political accountability or constraints. The combination of heavy taxation and PI policies, levied by Keynes who was the Advisor with Special Authority on Indian Financial and Monetary policy to the British Chancellor of the Exchequer and the Prime Minister, led to a decrease in the purchasing power of the wage earners which had a direct impact on their ability to buy and consume grains, leading to widespread deprivation. Deprivation which was left to turn into famine by continued resource consumption by Britain.

It is fair to say that Britain flourished off the backs of colonial deprivation and consequent death. Perhaps it still does. When Professor Patnaik's article was published in October, many of us who take interest in studying, teaching, or researching about colonialism were not entirely surprised. Maybe, reading about Keynes being directly connected to this colonial atrocity surprised us, but what was in no way surprising was the role of the British colonial enterprise in creating and exacerbating this historical crisis. For many of us, still dealing with the remnants of the colonial era in Britain and our now independent countries, the violence committed by the Raj and its agents is all too well remembered. While international coverage of this atrocity is sparse and un-nuanced; in my native country, India, every child learns of this atrocity and many others committed by the British in their history lessons at school.

History after all, plays a large part in memory, and the collective memory of Britain is suffering from a carefully crafted historical amnesia. The reason Keynes' involvement in the Bengal famine was surprising to many was not because we believed Keynes to be irreproachable, but because his connection with India and his involvement in the colonial project has been carefully edited by those that wrote biographies on him. Little space has been given to remember and memorialise the financial policies underlying the colonial rule that were created by Keynes and how India helped sustain the international gold standard and the impact on its economy due to the large forced loans that were taken from it.

Keynes, who played a central role in the creation of the Bretton Woods Institutions (today's World Bank and the International Monetary Fund), was a champion of liberal economics and the welfare state that was built off the nexus of colonialism and capitalism (Bhambra and Holmwood 2017); the machinations of liberal economics laid the stepping stones for neoliberal economics which has been co-opted by the World Bank and the IMF under their rhetoric of development. The implementation of these neoliberal schemes in the form of predatory loans and foreign direct investments in the Global South (previously ex-colonies) has contributed to land dispossession and exacerbated economic and social crises in these countries.[1]

Apart from his contribution to economics, Keynes was also an ardent supporter of eugenics and served as the director of the Eugenics Society from 1937 to 1944 (Singerman 2016). Keynes' commitment to eugenics deeply influenced his political and economic work, enthusiastically supporting contraception, as in his words 'it was essential because the working class was too drunken and ignorant to keep its numbers down' (Freedland 2012). Perhaps it is only coincidence that the same man who believed in an 'economic argument for population eugenics' was also responsible for the deaths of three million people. Nonetheless, these inherently racist ideas have sustained the Malthusian myth of 'overpopulation', insidiously contribute to economic and social marginalisation of non-white people and enable the rhetoric where immigrants are perceived to be competing with the 'natives' for resources and employment.

Decolonising this canon of Keynes requires us to re-examine our understanding and relationship with history — what we remember and how we remember it. To excuse the death of more than 3 million Bengali people and to paint the deprivation the region and the entire colony was under as 'an outcome of the war' is a patent lie. It creates an image that extraordinary times led to extraordinary measures which caused extraordinary atrocities; but famines, deaths, and deprivation were exceedingly ordinary in India during the time of colonial rule. When the British left in 1947, they left behind a country with 90% of its population living below the poverty line, literacy rate of 16%, and life expectancy at 27 years (Tharoor 2017). Similarly, to cast the horrors of Empire against perceived benign (or even 'helpful') contributions such as democracy, the rule of law, and lest we forget — the railways, is misleading.

Colonial projects do not set out to do 'good'; to discuss their benignity is to engage in sophistry.

Their primary motive is to exploit the colonised on behalf of the colonisers. To create a system so skewed where entire populations and their welfare is sentenced to invisibility while they, the colonisers, benefit from this invisibility. It is to create a system based on racist supremacy and violence and disguising it under policies and bureaucracy; left to be managed by people who are not proudly racist but believe that a skewed system is normal and are 'unwittingly' racist (Chaudhuri 2016). A colonial order is one that is institutionally racist, and the resurrection of this colonial order is increasingly visible in British society today making it difficult to view history with a sense of detached irony.

Institutions are made of people, and so when we talk of institutional racism, we are speaking about people's personal prejudices coming to the fore to collectively dictate policy. It is this transformation of personal prejudice into a well-established structure manned by both active proponents of racism and those that acquiesce, which makes the underhanded nature of institutional racism so difficult to grasp. Racism is not about individual morality, but in fact about the perpetuation and continued survival of systemic power differences. The continued existence of the systemic power difference between white and non-white people, which is further compounded along the axes of gender, socio-economic class, and migrant status is nowhere more starkly visible than in academia — a microcosm of British society.

British universities continue to remain 'ivory towers' in more than just a metaphorical sense. Majority of senior academic positions are held by white men (14,205 male professors, more than 12,000 are white), with only twenty-five black female senior academics across British universities (Higher Education Survey in Adams 2018). The issue of 'whiteness' in academia is deeply tied to representation of non-white people, or lack thereof. It is why the myth of 'BAME deficiency' has been so hard to budge and remains the top agenda of most Equality and Diversity Initiatives, which too are more often than not led by white people. It is disingenuous to suggest that the reason why black students are the highest proportion of UK students to score the lowest degree classification — a third or a pass — is due to a lack of intelligence, laziness, or lack of aspiration. It is more likely for black youth to go to university than it is for white youth, yet the structural disadvantage of not being white coupled with prejudicial attitudes of predominantly white staff perpetuates and exacerbates this 'attainment gap'. There is an image of what 'intelligence' and 'belonging' looks like in academia, and the image continues to perpetuate itself through the survival strategy of structural disadvantage of non-white people.

Perhaps one of the most pervasive myths after the 'BAME deficiency' myth is one that British universities are meritocratic and free from racism. The reality is far from this utopia that many Senior Managers at UK universities want to suggest. A recent *Guardian* investigation unveiled widespread evidence of discrimination in academia. The responses to freedom of information requests sent by *The Guardian* to 131 UK universities demonstrated that staff and students had made at least 996 formal complaints of racism over the past five years. Of this only a third were upheld (Batty 2019).

One wonders what the actual rate of complaints is, given how the investigation only looked at 'formal complaints' and did not include instances of Islamophobia and anti-Semitism. That university campuses across the UK are overtly and covertly hostile places for students and staff of colour is a fact that has been stated multiple times, previously and more forcefully now with students occupations and movements.[2] In such an environment that disables black and brown staff and students from thriving and belonging in the same manner as their white counterparts, the myth of meritocracy further harms us.

The invisibilisation of the structural disadvantages faced by people of colour at UK universities, squarely places the burden of undoing societal prejudice on our backs. In this Catch-22 situation, we either perish due to the prejudice or due to the impossible effort required to subvert them which we eventually fail to do as the goalposts keep shifting. Despite the existence of abundant proof that being a person of colour in Britain suggests that your life chances are obstructed at every point, up to 40% of British people believe that people of colour do not face discrimination — rising to 52% in the context of universities (Mohdin 2018). Any attempts to level the playing field is rendered impossible behind shouts of 'special treatment' and an acceleration of the 'political correctness agenda' (Eddo Lodge 2018, p. 73). This insistence on merit, suggesting that what has always been placed out of your reach — be it a first-class degree qualification or the promotion of female academics of colour to higher positions — can be obtained with just some good ol' fashioned hard work is facetious. It forgets that 'whiteness' in and of itself is synonymous with 'special treatment'. We would be foolish to continually internalise the myth of meritocracy, to our own detriment, when it is patently obvious that the unchanging presence of white men in the upper echelons of most professions is not simply due to their talent. It is due to their white privilege.

The unprecedented speed with which British society has given up on all notions of multiculturalism, to close ranks in favour of class and race in the past decade, but more visibly after Brexit; has disrupted the post-racial fantasy of 'multicultural and liberal Britain'. Many after Brexit, having seen the rising statistics in racial hate crime, muse 'I guess this is what Britain is now'.

But Britain has always been like this. As the UN Special Rapporteur on Racism concluded upon her visit to the UK in 2019, 'Brexit has not newly introduced racism and xenophobia to the United Kingdom — both have a long legacy that extends as far back as the historical European projects of slavery and colonialism.' From Enoch Powell's infamous 'Rivers of Blood' speech in 1960s, ramped up Islamophobia post-9/11, to Theresa May's tenure as Home Secretary that saw a tightening of immigration regulations and 'go back home' vans in predominantly immigrant neighbourhoods; shock over rising hate crime figures, as well-meaning as it is, forgets that British society has always been deeply hostile towards those that deviate from the established white norm.

The 'hostile environment' became par for the course in 2012 when it became part of Home Office policy towards 'illegal immigrants'. Motivated by a desire to bring down immigration numbers, Theresa May as Home Secretary told the Telegraph that her aim 'was to create here in Britain a really hostile environment for illegal migration.'[3] The policy empowered public institutions and agents such as hospitals, universities and even landlords to become immigration enforcement officers and impose heavy penalties were they to fail in their duties. It entrenched border controls into mundane activities such as visiting the doctor or renting a flat and soon became a pernicious form of surveillance.

Universities being among the public institutions tasked with enforcing this policy, have exacerbated institutional racism within their walls. The 'hostile environment' policy requires universities to comply with certain statutory duties towards non-EU students and staff. These are wide-ranging and can include ensuring that students meet an arbitrary set of contact hours, staff keep detailed attendance records of their students and ensure prior approval for any leave extending more than 10 days. In fact, Uni's Resist Border Controls (URBC 2018). A national campaigning group raising awareness about the hostile environment in UK universities states that there is a non-uniform practice of these 'statutory duties' with each university developing local policies to ensure compliance with 'monitoring' of non-EU international staff and students.

Ensuring compliance and carrying out these statutory duties is vitally important for UK universities if they want to continue hosting international students, who bring with them not just 'diversity' but also pay the hefty international students tuition fees which is an attractive source of income for cash-strapped universities. The significant risks of non-compliance have led to universities being stringent to the point that it penalises non-EU migrant staff and students. When errors are made by Home Office or university departments, it leaves migrant students and staff at risk of losing their right to remain in the UK which causes undue emotional distress.

Before even setting foot in the UK, non-EU migrants are expected to satisfy stringent immigration requirements of the Points Based Visa System, pay a hefty visa fees and an Immigrant Health Surcharge to contribute towards the National Health Service. In 2019, just the visa costs for a non-EU student pursuing a three-year undergraduate degree at a UK university is £1670.[4] Once in the UK, our undergraduate student can be expected to pay upwards of £12,000 for their degree (University of Oxford charges up to £34,000 in tuition fees for certain courses) and have limited opportunities for financial aid. Add to this, extortionate student accommodation fees, rising living costs, and punitive restrictions on part-time employment — seeking a degree in the UK becomes a financial nightmare for non-EU students and their families, especially for those coming from the Global South.

In such a system, non-EU staff and students suffer a unique precariousness which can be further compounded by institutional racism. For instance, between 2014 and 2016 almost 36,000 students from countries in South Asia had their Tier-4 student visas revoked for suspected cheating in an English language test centre (all of whom have now been cleared of any wrongdoing but still suffer from a disrupted life). In another case, student Ahmed Sedeeq[5] who is a PhD researcher at Sheffield, faced days of immigration detention in 2018 when his asylum claim was rejected and student visa was curtailed and even now is at risk of detention and deportation.

Such a strenuous impact of the hostile environment policy serves to kill knowledge and academic community in UK universities. It makes staff and students suspicious of each other and turns colleagues into border guards. It is known to have a significant impact on the mental health of migrants, creates an environment of fear, and prevents migrant students and staff from feeling like they belong in their universities and by extension in the UK. Unfortunately, studies and reports evaluating the international student experience in the UK are few and infrequent. It is also important to note that despite the structural problems that overseas students face at UK universities, there numbers have remained steady over the past few years.

UK universities are actively recruiting international students and dedicating resources towards 'internationalisation' strategies that include sending representatives to schools in non-European countries to hand out prospectuses and discuss course options. The neoliberal framework of UK universities has meant that they need to 'diversify' their portfolio of income generation, in such a situation non-EU student are a lucrative 'commodity'. Such a mind-set has led to the objectification of migrant students, where they're actively asked to participate in a system that is detrimental for them. The UK Council for International Student Affairs estimated that there were 312,660 non-EU students at UK universities in 2017, roughly 19% of the UK student population.[6]

To understand why students from outside the UK, especially those from the Global South, continue to come here and bear with the hostile environment; it is important we look at history. It is more than just a coincidence that UK universities are better resourced than their counterparts in the Global South. The spoils of colonialism and slavery are visible across British university campuses — Codrington Library at All Souls College (University of Oxford), the establishment of Owens College that is now University of Manchester, the £198 million endowment received by the University of Glasgow, majority of the funds that helped found University of Bristol — the list is endless.[7] It is perverse then, when a country and its universities built off the back of colonial and slave profits continue to extract profit from migrants while still being hostile towards us. As Ambalavaner Sivanandan said, 'we are here, because you were there' (Sivanandan, 2008).

The legacy of colonialism is still alive in universities, not just in the names of the buildings but the structural inequalities inherent in the system. As such I am not here to merely debate the merits of naming buildings after influential economists; the students of the Rhodes Must Fall campaign were not simply there to bring down the statue of Cecil Rhodes. To distil the very real concerns we harbour to simplistic questions of 'yes statute/no statue' is disingenuous. For us, the statues and bronze plaques commemorating the victories and contributions of these men — and they almost always are men — who society has designated as heroes and rendered them beyond criticism in the public eye, are a conduit to bring attention to the under-illuminated aspects of the British imperial project and the systemic inequality that people of colour and migrants still face. It is an inquiry not just into who these men were, but also an inquiry into whether we want to be the kind of society that uncritically remembers and memorialises such men. Accusing us of wanting to 'change' history, is facetious. We only aim to provide a complete picture of it, one that is not viewed through the rose tinted glasses of glorious Britannia.

When we speak of the decolonial, a term that runs the risk of being opaque and difficult to translate out of the theoretical, we speak simply of improving the representation of non-white non-European people, our histories, our languages, and our heterogeneity. The project of decoloniality is a project of self-determination, wherein we seek to end the misrepresentation that our native non-European cultures only began from the colonial encounter — that our lands and we were 'found' by a Christopher Columbus or a Vasco De Gama. It is to extricate ourselves from the stereotypical image created of us by the white establishment, which many of us have internalised. To decolonise is to reclaim our own agency.

Decolonising academia has to mean more than just a 'diverse' curriculum or fallen monuments. It has to be reflective of what the impact of the structural inequalities is on those that grapple with them most. It requires us to acknowledge the fact that the system is colonial to begin with, and through that ask questions of what being part of a colonial system means. It needs us to disrupt the idea that some belong less at the university due to their race, class, gender, and migrant status. A decolonial academy is one that dismantles structural privilege and resists against forces of inequality.

Yet, when privilege has so many platforms — furthered by globalisation — the task of decolonisation becomes a complex matter. I return here, to Keynes and his role in furthering the institutions that has made it possible for free-market globalisation to continue unrestrained. The growth of the free-market has empowered the rich by normalising the capacity to earn large amounts of capital and made it a measure of success. Alongside, globalisation has opened up the free-market and its associated largesse to economies that were excluded in colonial times.

In Britain, beneficiaries of this free-market globalisation can trade not just in material wealth but other forms of capital such as networks, name, class, and race. Yet, names, class, networks, and race are inextricably linked to colonial legacies, which get 'capital' value ascribed to them through these free-market designs. As such, attempts to constrain this particular 'capital' is seen as unwelcome, but all constraints can be done away when the 'capital' is turned into something which is a 'common inheritance' of the British people — for all to benefit from (obviously not those who question the validity of this capital). This way, the legacy of the empire is whitewashed and all representations of it — material or otherwise — become family heirlooms to be cherished and protected at all cost with immense sentimental and cultural value (Chaudhuri 2016). But what happens when those who expected to profit off this legacy, fail to do so? It leads us to where we are today.

The social capital of being 'British' that many had hoped would lead them to accessing prosperity, has been increasingly devalued by the same free market globalisation that ascribed them value in the first place. The resentment that lies at the root of the 'immigrants stealing jobs' brigade is simply this — a misplaced belief that by being white and British (and conflating one with the other) they are simply better and more deserving, and when this misplaced belief does not yield fruit, they hark back to Ye Olde Days where 'all was good'. The current state of British society is a direct result of its reluctance to address its history in full, including the inglorious parts of Britannia.

The absence of regret and wilful blindness towards the violence colonialism really entailed contributes to the institutionally racist country and society that Britain continues to be. But this is not an issue constrained specifically to Britain and has come to define the boundaries of the world we live, work, and travel in. The resurrected colonial order is stacked against the non-European, and finds increasing justification for itself in the post-9/11 world, with the new mission of preserving its 'way of life and civilisation', a sly inversion of the original colonial mission. This reconfiguration creates a persistent asymmetry where the affairs of Aleppo, Tehran, and Dhaka are not worthy of notice (and even when affairs occurring there are noticed it is only those that are violent and have implications in the Global North) and do not have a way of life; unlike London, Paris and New York where any event must make international headlines and be of international significance.

This is about more than just monuments, changing the name of Keynes

College or bringing down the statue of Rhodes and other colonialists across Britain will not protect minorities from suffering under the more insidious, quieter form of imperialism. The systemic racism that prevents students of colour from getting a place at Oxbridge, promotes young black men being stopped and searched on the streets, or the enhanced checking of brown and black people at airports will continue to exist. The legacy of the Empire will not necessarily be less malevolent just because it will be rendered less visible. It is easier to take down a statue than it is to tell people who aren't manifestly racist but still riddled with unconscious bias that their beliefs and behaviour facilitate oppression.

If we are to truly confront the rot of institutional racism, then the crimes of the Empire must be faced up to. A frank discussion must be had about the shameful moments that make up colonial history and their generational ramifications on people of colour in the UK but also on ex-British colonies. Today, when white supremacy is resurgent once again and white racial anxieties of a 'white genocide' are being legitimised by a quota of academics at British universities,[8] it is imperative that the myopia of white privilege is reckoned with. Those who, after Brexit, are now feeling the heat of the hostile environment and the inequalities that people of colour in Britain have felt for decades need to evaluate the blinders that they have lived with for so long and listen to the voices continually silenced.

We need to undertake a critical, honest reflection on history if our future is to be ethical. Trying to deny or escape past legacies has calamitous effects on the future for anyone concerned with living in an equitable society. In academia, this is impossible to do unless we understand how systemic inequalities of the macro are reproduced and intensified in the micro. Simply increasing diversity in staff and students and implementing short-term 'inclusion programmes' without actively dismantling structural hurdles exposes already vulnerable and marginalised people to more of the same violent forces of inequality. As Karen Salt (2019) suggests, we cannot keep planting trees and hoping them to turn out healthy when the soil is toxic; instead we must ask ourselves 'what is in the soil?'

Decolonising in such an environment also requires us to think about a sustainable form of survival, for ourselves, without fetishising decolonisation and resisting its co-option by the wider machinery. For this, as we look outwards at the memorialisation of history and its contemporary manifestations, we must also look inwards and self-reflect on how we have internalised historical representations of ourselves (Akala 2018). Deconstructing our internal biases about ourselves necessitates honesty and accountability, which in their discomfort can create space for understanding and undoing oppressive thoughts we hold in ourselves. The introspection is also important to disrupt the 'oppressor/oppressed' binary, wherein the systemic difficulties faced by us make us blind to the privileges we hold on to. Undoing this binary is an important step towards self-actualisation in undoing oppressive institutional structures and being allies.

Transforming the toxic space in this manner, relies on empathy and humanity as praxis in decolonising. It moves the conversation beyond the classroom and engages with the lived experiences of not just the students and teaching staff but also cleaners, security, kitchen staff, and administrators. Creating our own epistemological frameworks for not just engaging with texts and 'in-class' activities but also with conversations outside enables us in creating a mode of knowledge-production that displaces known pedagogies and is collaborative. It gives you and the person or object or place you are interacting with a stake in the final output. It makes knowledge and by extension the site where that knowledge is produced, personal.

Embodying decoloniality in the present, instead of constraining it to sporadic moments is how we move towards an ethical university based on equitable principles. Undoing the everyday onslaught of institutional racism and other structural inequalities calls for cultivating an everyday decolonial. Here and now. On our terms.

## Notes

1 For further discourse on the analysis of the processes of globalisation and the resulting emergence of the global economy please refer to Peet R. (2003). *Unholy Trinity: The IMF, World Bank, and WTO*. New York: Zed Books.

2 For a well written overview of the history of student occupations against racism at UK universities see: Gbagbo E. (6 January 2020). The History of Anti-Racist Student Occupation Movements in the UK. *Gal-Dem Magazine*. https://gal-dem.com/what-we-need-to-learn-about-the-history-of-anti-racist-student-occupation-movements-in-the-uk/.

3 You can read the full interview here: Kirkup J and Winett R (25 May 2012). 'Theresa May Interview: "We're Going to Give Illegal Migrants a Really Hostile Reception"'. *The Telegraph*. https://www.telegraph.co.uk/news/uknews/

immigration/9291483/Theresa-May-interview-Were-going-to-give-illegal-migrants-a-really-hostile-reception.html.

4  According to current costs, the immigrant health surcharge for 3 years costs £1350 and the fees for a regular tier 4 visa application is £320.

5  For further information on this case see reporting on: BBC England (2018). Ahmed Sedeeq: Thousands Back Iraqi student's PhD Bid. https://www.bbc.co.uk/news/uk-england-south-yorkshire-42611915.

6  For a further breakdown by domicile, level of study and mode of study, consult the tables in the report: UK Council for International Student Affairs (2019). International Student Statistics: UK Higher Education. https://www.ukcisa.org.uk/Research--Policy/Statistics/International-student-statistics-UK-higher-education.

7  For further detail on how certain UK Universities profited from their links to colonialism and slavery, read: (30 April 2019). How Have British Universities Grappled With Links to the Slave Trade? *Reuters*, World News. https://www.reuters.com/article/us-britain-slavery-universities-factbox/how-have-british-universities-grappled-with-links-to-the-slave-trade-idUSKCN1S61TX.

8  For a good analysis and rebuttal of the argument of 'White Genocide' being legitimised by a minority of academics please read: Trilling D. (April 2019). I'm Not Racist But ... . *London Review of Books* 41(8), pp. 19–22. https://www.lrb.co.uk/v41/n08/daniel-trilling/im-not-racist-but.

## References

Adams, R. (2018). UK Universities Making Slow Progress on Equality, Data Shows. *The Guardian*, Higher Education. Available from: https://www.theguardian.com/education/2018/sep/07/uk-university-professors-black-minority-ethnic.

Akala. (2018). *Natives: Race and Class in the Ruins of Empire*. London, United Kingdom: Two Roads Books.

Batty, D. (2019). UK Universities Condemned for Failure to Tackle Racism. *The Guardian*, Universities. Available from: https://www.theguardian.com/education/2019/jul/05/uk-universities-condemned-for-failure-to-tackle-racism.

Bhambra, G. K. and Holmwood, J. (2017). Colonialism, Postcolonialism and the Liberal Welfare State. *New Political Economy* 23, 574–587. Available from: https://doi.org/10.1080/13563467.2017.1417369.

Chaudhuri, A. (2016). The Real Meaning of Rhodes Must Fall. *The Guardian*. The Long Read. Available from: https://www.theguardian.com/uk-news/2016/mar/16/the-real-meaning-of-rhodes-must-fall.

Eddo-Lodge, R. (2018). *Why I'm No Longer Talking to White People about Race.*

London, United Kingdom: Bloomsbury.

Freedland, J. (2012). Eugenics: The Skeleton That Rattles Loudest in the Left's Closet. *The Guardian*, Opinion. Available from: https://www.theguardian.com/commentisfree/2012/feb/17/eugenics-skeleton-rattles-loudest-closet-left.

Gbagbo, E. (2020) The History of Anti-Racist Student Occupation Movements in the UK. *Gal-Dem Magazine*, Politics. Available from: https://gal-dem.com/what-we-need-to-learn-about-the-history-of-anti-racist-student-occupation-movements-in-the-uk/.

Kirkup, J. and Winett R. (2012). 'Theresa May Interview: "We're Going to Give Illegal Migrants a Really Hostile Reception"'. *The Telegraph*. Available from: https://www.telegraph.co.uk/news/uknews/immigration/9291483/Theresa-May-interview-Were-going-to-give-illegal-migrants-a-really-hostile-reception.html.

Mohdin, A. (20 December 2018). Up to 40% of Britons Think Bame People Do Not Face More Discrimination. *The Guardian*, Race. Available from: https://www.theguardian.com/world/2018/dec/20/up-to-40-of-britons-think-bame-people-do-not-face-more-discrimination.

Patnaik, U. (2017). MR Keynes and the Forgotten Holocaust in Bengal, 1943–44: Or, the Macroeconomics of Extreme Demand Compression. *Studies in People's History* 4(2), pp. 197– 210. Available from: https://doi.org/10.1177/2348448917725856.

Patnaik, U. (2018) Profit Inflation, Keynes and the Holocaust in Bengal 1943–44. *Economic and Political Weekly* 53. Available from; https://www.epw.in/journal/2018/42/special-articles/profit-inflation-keynes-and-holocaust.html.

Peet, R. (2003). *Unholy Trinity: The IMF, World Bank, and WTO*. New York: Zed Books.

Reuters (2019). How Have British Universities Grappled With Links to the Slave Trade? *Reuters*, World News. Available from: https://www.reuters.com/article/us-britain-slavery-universities-factbox/how-have-british-universities-grappled-with-links-to-the-slave-trade-idUSKCN1S61TX.

Salt, K. (2019). Keynote Talk at Decolonising the University of Kent Conference. Available from: https://www.youtube.com/watch?v=KYglXKq7yJ4&t=97s.

Sedeeq, A. (2018). Thousands Back Iraqi Student's PhD Bid. BBC England. Available from: https://www.bbc.co.uk/news/uk-england-south-yorkshire-42611915.

Singerman, D. (2016). Keynesian Eugenics and the Goodness of the World. *Journal of British Studies*, 55(3), pp. 538–565. Available from: https://doi:10.1017/jbr.2016.56.

Sivanandan, A. (2008). *Catching History on The Wing*. London: Pluto Press.

Tharoor, S. (2017). 'But What About the Railways ...?' The Myth of Britain's Gifts to India. *The Guardian*, Colonialism. Available from: https://www.theguardian.

com/world/2017/mar/08/india-britain-empire-railways-myths-gifts.

Trilling, D. (April 2019). I'm Not Racist But .... *London Review of Books* 41(8), 19–22 Available from: https://www.lrb.co.uk/v41/n08/daniel-trilling/im-not-racist-but.

UK Council for International Student Affairs. (2019) International Student Statistics: UK Higher Education [Online]. Available from: https://www.ukcisa. org.uk/Research--Policy/Statistics/International-student-statistics-UK-higher-education.

Unis Resist Border Controls (2018). The 'Hostile Environment', Racism, and the Value of Migrants in UK Universities. *USS Briefs*. Available from: https:// medium.com/ussbriefs/the-hostile-environment-racism-and-the-value-of-migrants-in-uk-universities-80d988b6a093.

United Nations Office of the High Commissioner for Human Rights. (2019). United Kingdom: UN Expert Condemns Entrenched Racial Discrimination and Inequality [Online]. *Office of the High Commissioner of Human Rights*, News. Available from: https://www.ohchr.org/EN/NewsEvents/Pages/DisplayNews. aspx?NewsID=24698&LangID=E.

§3

# STANDING ON OUR SHOULDERS: ACADEMICS OF COLOUR EMPOWERING STUDENT CHANGE AGENTS

3

# Zine-Making for Anti-Racist Learning and Action

*Building the Anti-Racist Classroom*
*https://barcworkshop.org/*

## Who We Are and How We Work

Building the Anti-racist Classroom (BARC) is an international collective of women of colour scholar-activists. We found each other gradually through a number of events within the critical margins of business and management studies. We were drawn to one another through a shared interest in working to make space for ourselves and our work, which means resisting the white patriarchal Anglo/Eurocentrism that dominates our teaching, research and learning environments. The business management field consistently centres whiteness and masculinity, and plays a key role in uncritically reproducing neo-colonialist ideologies that privilege white bodies not only at the local level of higher education institutions, but globally through the legitimacy, influence and reach of its knowledge production. The role of our discipline is significant given the large and growing numbers of students that business and management schools take in year-on-year, and the reliance of universities on this income from student fees. For these reasons, we actively work towards transforming higher education by theorising our conditions, developing strategic interventions, and building community through centring people of colour.

We are guided by the work of a long line of anti-racist thinkers whose ideas and interventions have formed the foundation of contemporary feminist, critical race, and postcolonial and w frameworks.[1] Recognising the history of anti-racist work is an important keystone enabling us to

challenge whiteness with a sense of responsibility and self-accountability, and to start to re-narrate institutional histories and unveil how
they have been shaped by racism and imperialism. The re-connection
of past, present and future in anti-racist work means that it is essential
to introduce more people of colour into positions of voice and power.
We seek to create principled spaces facilitating this: centering curiosity,
vulnerable reflection, respectful learning, transformation and liberation.[2]
In these spaces, we adopt a structural and institutional analytical lens,
disrupting the individual focus of neoliberal narratives and refusing to
victim-blame. In these ways, we actively work against the deficit model
within higher education.

Our anti-racist work is rooted in the belief that the transformation
of higher education is only possible as a collective endeavour: we have
formed close connections with, and have been supported by, many
people beyond our core organising collective, including the students
and facilitators of Decolonise UKC. We thank them for embracing us,
challenging us, and inviting us to grow alongside them. We continually
seek to become and remain humble and vulnerable in our own reflexive
learning as we do this work. A striving for solidaristic practice means we
must ground our work in a radical practice of self-deferment, following
the lead and the needs of the most marginalised. We are committed to an
anti-racist pedagogy that makes space for forms of knowledge that have
been marginalised from the mainstream. Our work has therefore been
led by art, activism and affect: engaging with embodied knowledge, lived
experiences, practices and people from outside business and management, and beyond the university, to challenge what (and who) is valued.

**Zine-Making with Decolonise UKC**

We were honoured to be invited to contribute to the Decolonise UKC[3]
manifesto launch, and designed a 'zine'-making session to encourage
the staff in attendance to engage with the demands of the manifesto
and to facilitate them in considering how they could support it through
a set of actions. We have found such artistic methodologies helpful in
intervening in traditional academic spaces that constrain certain forms
of knowledge and bodies. For this workshop we were inspired specifically
by a young woman activist who presented at the 'Black Cultural Activism
Map' event in London, sharing the zines she made on the issue of ending
the hostile environment for immigration.[4]

The term 'zine' is thought to emerge from 'fanzine' and represents a practice that has been around for centuries. They are a low-cost, non-commercial, and accessible form of alternative media. Zines facilitate the challenging of dominant narratives in mainstream media, the connecting of people with shared interests and commitments, and are thus a form of social action, carving out space for new sociabilities, and holding the potential to contribute to counter-hegemonic transformation. Making and disseminating zines means taking an active part in cultural production; since rising in popularity among punk communities in the 1970s and queer and feminist groups in the 1990s, zines have experienced a resurgence and relevance in the digital age (see Ramdarshan Bold 2017). Yet, print-based zines also appear continue to offer a mode of self- and community-making for people of colour on our own terms.[5] Representing the most un-mediated, personal, medium for people of colour to communicate the truth of their experiences, zines are an important resource in anti-racist pedagogy (Latif and Jeppsen 2007).

The zine-making session at the launch of the Decolonise UoK manifesto was the second of two events facilitated by BARC. It was primed and informed by a workshop held in the weeks prior to the launch, hosted at Queen Mary University London (QMUL). Students from both Kent and QMUL came together to work on developing anti-racist and decolonising strategy through collaborative creative practice. We brought along examples of zines, imagery, and art materials, and the students engaged in peer-to-peer education to explore what interventions and alternative futures might look like for their institutions. Through this process, the inter-institutional community of students created and consolidated ideas that informed the subsequent workshop for staff at the launch of the Decolonise University of Kent manifesto, including the notion of the 'Kaleidoscope Hub':

> A principled community space where students of colour feel able to access and develop strong networks of support and sense of belonging and find help to deal with racialisation on campus. (Decolonise University of Kent Manifesto)

After a brief introduction to the collective and its work, we invited staff at the launch event to think through what the Decolonise University of Kent manifesto might mean in practice. Using a series of prompts building upon the manifesto content and designed to help participants think through stages from reflection to action, we pre-printed a zine for people to cut & fold, write on, and take away. The zine was structured in four parts, book-ended by an outline of what decolonising work means, guidance on how to use the zine, and a list of further resources.

*Part one — 'The colour of our curriculum'*

This page of the zine prompted staff to think through:

- I feel included when ...
- Cultural democracy in higher education looks like ...
- I/We can centre people of colour in teaching and learning by ...

By thinking about their own experiences of feeling *included*, we hoped that white staff in particular would reflect on the extent to which spaces in higher education are designed by default to include them before turning outwards to consider what these spaces might look like if they centred people of colour in classrooms, curricula, practices, and policies.

*Part two — Kaleidoscope Hub*

This page of the zine asked staff to imagine the construction of an alternative space:

- Write a word or draw an image that symbolises an inclusive space of learning and community-building

This activity sought to concretise and turn the ideas and commitments developed on the first page into action and ongoing practice.

*Part Three — Student Voice*

This page of the zine encouraged staff to recall and record what they had heard that day:

- Think about what students of colour have said today. Write a memorable quote.

By asking participants to focus on the many voices of students that had been expressed at the event and to select one quote, we sought to reflect on, elevate and retain this knowledge.

*Part Four — Pledge-Writing*

This part of the zine asked staff to continue thinking and acting beyond the session:

• We encourage you to read the manifesto and make a personal pledge to support it in your own teaching and learning, and work with Decolonise UKC to realise its aims. A pledge is not:

    ○ A tick-box exercise;
    ○ To make you feel or look good!

Your pledge should be focused on: empowering students of colour, and collectively with people of colour, challenging structures that prevent students and staff of colour from progressing in higher education.

This final element of the zine not only oriented the exercise into personal commitment as an individual or team, but also sought to acknowledge two pitfalls that occur frequently in decolonising work: neutralisation by inaction and co-optation for individual gain.

We closed the session by encouraging staff to take their completed zines with them and to disseminate them:

• Spread the message! Zines are low-tech communication tools that can be easily created and shared. Fold them up and place them in unexpected places e.g. university library books and brochure holders.

• **You can** photocopy this template and give it to friends, classmates, strangers, lecturers, Heads of School.
• **You can** work together to hold a zine-making workshop and create your own template, designs and messages for change.

The flip side of the zine was also designed as a poster that could be hung up in staff offices, indicating a commitment to support the Decolonise UoK manifesto. We encourage staff, student and activist groups to experiment with taking the zine format into your own classrooms,

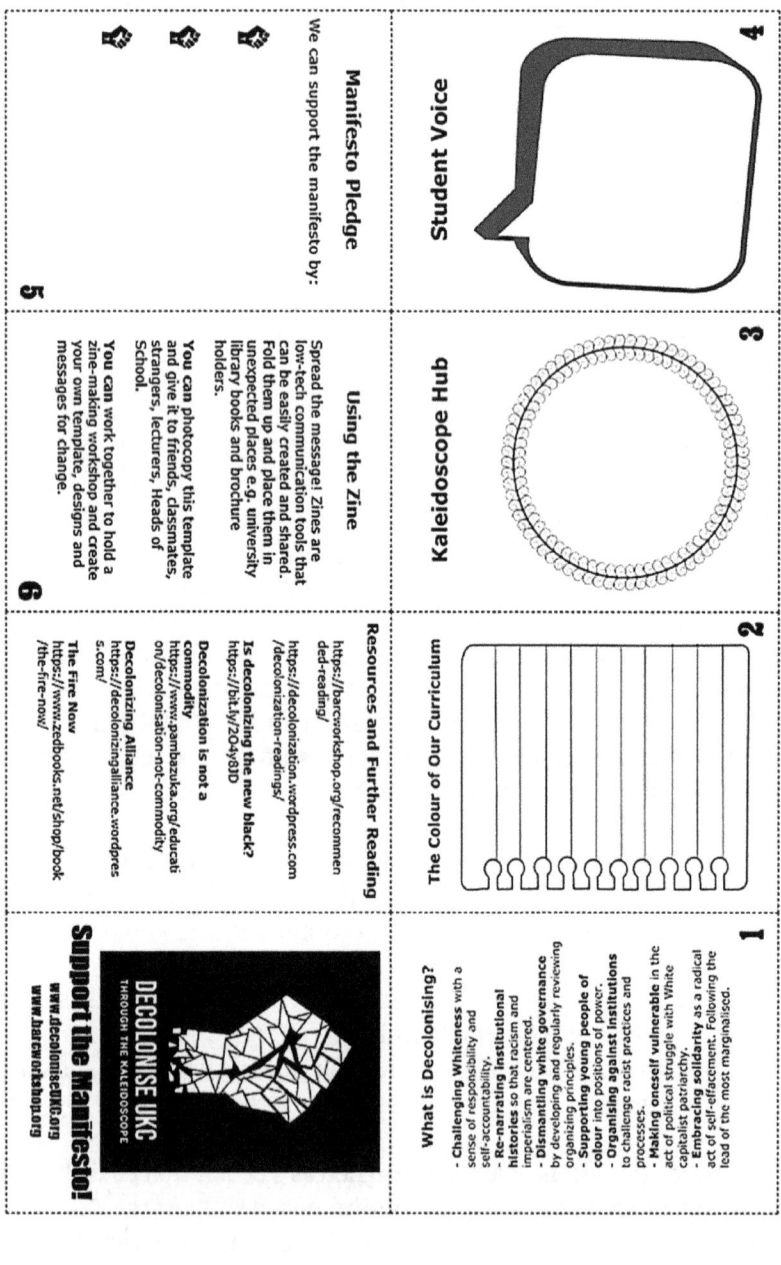

**4**

## Student Voice

**5**

## Manifesto Pledge

We can support the manifesto by:

**3**

## Kaleidoscope Hub

## Using the Zine

Spread the message! Zines are low-tech communication tools that can be easily created and shared. Fold them up and place them in unexpected places e.g. university library books and brochure holders.

**You can** photocopy this template and give it to friends, classmates, strangers, lecturers, Heads of School.

**You can** work together to hold a zine-making workshop and create your own template, designs and messages for change.

**6**

**2**

## The Colour of Our Curriculum

## Resources and Further Reading

https://barcworkshop.org/recommended-reading/

https://decolonization.wordpress.com/decolonization-reading/

**Is decolonizing the new black?** https://bit.ly/2O4y8JD

**Decolonization is not a commodity** https://www.pambazuka.org/education/decolonisation-not-commodity

**Decolonizing Alliance** https://decolonizingalliance.wordpres s.com/

**The Fire Now** https://www.zedbooks.net/shop/book /the-fire-now/

**1**

## What is Decolonising?

- **Challenging Whiteness** with a sense of responsibility and self-accountability.
- **Re-narrating institutional** histories so that racism and imperialism are centered.
- **Dismantling white governance** by developing and regularly reviewing organizing principles.
- **Supporting young people of colour** into positions of power.
- **Organising against institutions** to challenge racist practices and processes.
- **Making oneself vulnerable** in the act of political struggle with White capitalist patriarchy.
- **Embracing solidarity** as a radical act of self-effacement. Following the lead of the most marginalised.

**Support the Manifesto!**
www.decoloniseukc.org
www.barcworkshop.org

**DECOLONISE UKC**
THROUGH THE KALEIDOSCOPE

organising zine making sessions as a way to document and disseminate the alternative knowledges you develop.

## Notes

1 See for example, our reading list: https://barcworkshop.org/recommended-reading/.

2 Learn more about the principled space: https://barcworkshop.org/resources/principled-space/.

3 The group was formerly known as 'Decolonise UKC' (University of Kent at Canterbury) as appears in Figure 1 before its remit was broadened to a cross-university project.

4 See the event details here: http://stuarthallfoundation.org/what-we-do/events/launch-of-black-cultural-activism-map/.

5 See for example: https://www.artsy.net/article/artsy-editorial-8-zines-people-color-medium-remained-relevant.

## References

Decolonise UKC (2019). Decolonising the Curriculum: Through the Kaleidoscope, Manifesto. Available at: https://padletuploads.storage.googleapis.com/365414657/4fa7db651d36836670fec5ae9b5e8002/decolonising_the_curriculum_manifesto.pdf.

Latif, A. & Jeppesen, S. (2007). Toward an Anti-Authoritarian Anti-Racist Pedagogy. In: Shukaitis, W., Graeber, D. and Biddle, E. eds. *Constituent Imagination: Militant Investigations/Collective Theorization*. Edinburgh: AK Press, pp. 288–300.

Ramdarshan-Bold, M. (2017). Why Diverse Zines Matter: A Case Study of the People of Color Zines Project. *Publishing Research Quarterly* 33(3), pp. 215–228.

———

Further information about contemporary POC zines, and recommendations, from:

*Bitchmedia*: https://www.bitchmedia.org/post/cut-paste-five-black-zine-lives.

*Medium*: https://medium.com/@trodgersjohns/how-women-of-colour-are-manufacturing-their-own-representation-using-zines-b6f2e73ba0db.

*VICE*: https://www.vice.com/en_us/article/4xqkdd/brown-paper-zine-small-press-fair.

*UK and Ireland Zine Librarians*: https://uizl.wordpress.com/uk-and-ireland-zine-libraries-directory/.

# Decolonising the University of Kent: Where It Still Must Go and What It Still Must Be

*Dave S.P. Thomas*
*University of Kent*

Have we been waiting to be accepted for so long that not being accepted has become the criteria for acceptance?

(Lemn Sissay 2017, xxi)

The emergence of student-led campaigns such as '#Why is My Curriculum White?' and 'Rhodes Must Fall' has resulted in universities valorising movements to 'decolonise' education as a means of evidencing their commitment to achieve progress on equality for underrepresented groups to succeed and progress in higher education (Advance Higher Education 2019; OfS 2019a) and signal their intentions as 'a major business and revenue generator' (Hubble, Foster and Bolton 2016; OfS 2019b). But to what extent can the 'master's tools' be fashioned to perpetuate an unequal status quo (Lorde 1984) truly redress structural inequalities promoted and maintained by the legacy of colonialism? Professor John Henrik Clarke[1] proclaimed,

history is a compass that people use to find themselves on the map of human geography. The role of history is to tell people what they have been, where they have been ... where they still must go and what they still must be.

Before we explore where we still must go and what we still must be, we must establish where we have been by acknowledging the contributions of black scholars at the University of Kent who attempted to introduce Black Studies through courses on African history and black studies ideas as a means of decolonising education in the 1970s. Still, almost five decades later, the conversations and endeavours continue through the operationalisation of black intellectual capital as a 'pedagogy of hope' (Thomas 2019) and the amplification of the student voices through the #DecoloniseUoK movement and subsequent manifesto. But how did we get to this moment? What has been?

A moment can only be understood by placing it within a wider historical and structural context. Within the academe, this structural and historical context has served to normalise structural inequalities. Dr Jason Arday, speaking on the culture in UK higher education maintained that racial microaggression has become a vector through which much of the insidious racism that transpires throughout the contemporary academe is transmitted. It then does not come as a surprise that Lord Robbins, in stating his fourth aim of higher education declared:

> Once the reserve of the privileged few, higher education ... now [has] to perform a role in ameliorating social inequalities in an age that has set for itself 'the ideal of equality of opportunity. (Robbins 1963)

Still, where must we still go? Students are becoming more culturally and politically cognisant, demanding a re-curation of their curricula to redress its narrow perspectives which are fuelled by epistemic injustice, epistemic violence and a narcissistic desire to maintain exclusionary structures. Professor Robbie Shilliam highlighting the frailties of the imperial academy implored that epistemic justice calls for a reckoning with the racialised inequalities of knowledge cultivation that have historically accompanied the European colonial project (Shilliam 2019). Hence, if we are to decolonise the exclusionary spaces and structures of the academe in these times of explicit racial and epistemic violence, we need to establish where we still must go and what we still can be. We need to have a clear understanding of what it means to decolonise. The process of decolonisation is uncomfortable and inconvenient. It is a process of disorder that requires a critical approach to dismantling and displacing hegemonic structures. Decolonisation is not an addendum. Decolonisation is not a metaphor. Eve Tuck and Wayne Yang explicates the process of decolonisation. They argue that

> decolonization is not a metaphor. When metaphor invades decolonization, it kills the very possibility of decolonization; it recenters whiteness, it resettles theory, it extends innocence to the settler, it entertains a settler future. Decolonise (a verb) and decolonization (a noun) cannot easily be

grafted onto pre-existing discourses/frameworks, even if they are critical, even if they are anti-racist, even if they are justice frameworks. The easy absorption, adoption, and transposing of decolonization is yet another form of settler appropriation. When we [talk] about decolonization, we are not offering it as a metaphor; it is not an approximation of other experiences of oppression. Decolonization is not a swappable term for other things we want to do to improve our societies and [institutions of learning]. Decolonization doesn't have a synonym. (Tuck and Yang 2012, p. 3)

Therefore, decolonising education requires a decolonial transformation, organised and underscored by a critical race methodology and social justice imperatives, in order to redress structural inequality in the academe. It requires a relationship with the past and an appetite to become a part of living history, in order to de-link Eurocentrism from epistemic justice. It requires faculty and the institutions to proactively undergo the uncomfortable process of self-reflection. If we are to transform the academe and ameliorate the 'others' from their narratively and epistemically condemned status, we need to refashion the master's tools! We need a reconsideration of power relations (Thomas 2020) and an examination of the production of history that has brought us to the present. History is about intellectual integrity. We need to reimagine what we still must be — a higher education space that involve and include multiple stakeholders in a welcoming, inclusive environment where students are held to high expectations in order to achieve their maximum potential.

Students at the University of Kent are now creating history and suggesting where the univ ersity still must go through a series of recommendations, as laid out in their *Manifesto*. As a 'bottom up' approach, this has to be supported by allies and senior management in order to effect sustainable change. It is important to recognise that white guilt may result as part of this tumultuous process; this should not be the aim of the movement. In the words of George Yancy,

guilt can be deployed productively; it need not result in an emotional dead-end … one benefit of [the decolonising the university of Kent movement] should be to get white people to see how whiteness prevents them from becoming more deeply concerned about what it means to be human outside a [university] that stipulates whiteness as normative. (Yancy and Del Guadalupe Davidson 2016, p. 12).

This has now become a call to action at the University of Kent in order to shape a vision of where the university still MUST go and what it still MUST be!

## Notes

1  Quoted in Anthony T. Browder (1992), *Nile Valley Contributions to Civilisation*. Washington DC: US Institute of Karmic Guidance, p. 29.

## References

Advance HE (2019). Equality Charters Explained [Online]. Available at: https://www.ecu.ac.uk/equality-charters/charter-marks-explained/.

Hubble, S., Foster, D. and Bolton, P. (2016). Higher Education and Research Bill, Research Briefing. [Online]. Available at: https://researchbriefings.parliament.uk/ResearchBriefing/Summary/CBP-7608.

Lorde, A. (1984). *Sister Outsider*. Berkley, CA: Crossing Press.

OfS, (2019a). Access and Participation Plans [Online]. Available at: https://www.officeforstudents.org.uk/advice-and-guidance/promoting-equal-opportunities/access-and-participation-plans/.

OfS, (2019b). Fee Limits [Online]. Available at: https://www.officeforstudents.org.uk/advice-and-guidance/promoting-equal-opportunities/access-and-participation-plans/fee-limits/.

Robbins, C. (1963). The Report of the Committee Appointed by the Prime Minister under the Chairmanship of Lord Robbins.

Shilliam, R. (2019). Behind the Rhodes Statue: Black Complacency and the Imprial Academy. *History of Human Sciences* xx, pp. 1–25.

Sissay, L. (2017). *Gold from the Stone*. Edinburgh, UK: Cannongate Books.

Thomas, D. (2020). Belonging for 'Outsiders Within', A Critical Race Perspective on Whiteness as a Means of Promoting the 'Insider Without' Syndrome. Encyclopedia of Teacher Education [Online]: 1–5. Available at: https://link.springer.com/content/pdf/10.1007%2F978-981-13-1179-6_372-1.pdf.

Thomas, D. (2019). Black Intellectual Capital: Towards a 'Pedagogy of Hope' [Online]. Available at: https://www.advance-he.ac.uk/news-and-views/Black-Intellectual-Capital-Towards-a-pedagogy-of-hope.

Tuck, E. and Yang, W.K. (2012). Decolonization Is Not a Metaphor. *Decolonization: Indigeneity, Education & Society* 1, pp. 1–40.

Yancy, G. and Del Guadalupe Davidson, M. (2016). Thinking About Race, History and Identity: An Interview With George Yancy. *The Western Journal of Black Studies* 40.

# 5

# Doing Diversity Work with Students

*Dr Barbara Adewumi*
*University of Kent*

Decolonization never takes place unnoticed for it influences individuals and modifies them fundamentally'.

(Fanon 2005, p. 35)

Decolonising the curriculum in the academy proves to be an intellectually and institutionally complex matter that needs to be addressed with changes in pedagogical practices within the colonial curriculum. There needs to be cross-party collaboration supported by leadership teams committed to the cause — this is where the power lies in terms of changing traditional institutional cultures that will disrupt processes with progressive and inclusive interventions for social justice. Commitment to change also lies within faculties and programmes where academics interact with students in seminars, lecture theatres and around campuses. I am one of those academics who is trying to do the right thing within the white spaces of academia alongside our Black, Asian and minority ethnic (BAME) students, who I believe provide valuable insight into the embodiment of colonised literature by becoming co-producers of knowledge and co-actors of change.

As Decolonising the Curriculum campaign at the University of Kent[1] gained momentum, more and more I began to critically reflect on my teaching and the engagement with my students. It became more apparent to me as an academic immersed in social theory, that my earlier undergraduate forms of knowledge experience was shaped by Western education. I too needed to question my own implicit Eurocentrism(s) to more precisely construct and cultivate pedagogies that actively destabilise Eurocentric norms.

My first-year students are taught 'classic' forms of knowledge in sociology. They become all too familiar with the 'founding fathers of sociological theory.' The white elite philosophers of knowledge. Such concepts and views are acknowledged by the university's recommended reading on various reading lists. Such forms of knowledge are structured in a way that it becomes normal — as natural as breathing in air. So as BAME students *inhale* Eurocentric ideologies there is never a moment to *exhale* and see oneself amongst valued scholarship because global South and BAME authors remain largely unacknowledged within the curriculum. Subsequently, I have felt the need to actively challenge the assumptions of the global North, be critical of power dynamics in knowledge production and question structural inequalities reflected in pedological practices and leading academic scholarship.

Whilst teaching in the academy, I have embarked on a project which reviews social sciences school's reading lists known as the Reading List Review (otherwise called the Diversity Mark Project). Others feel slightly surprised as to what has been achieved so far and question how I've been able to do so much on the project which is over and above all teaching commitments. I secured two rounds of university funding and the project has since won the Tails Aspire award for its collaborative staff-student lead contribution to diversifying the reading material towards decolonising the curriculum.

Through the Review of the Reading list project, the apparent white male dominance of the reading lists has initiated a conversation between staff and students about how predominantly Eurocentric the reading lists actually are and how this does not reflect the student body. The project provided an opportunity to develop a wider debate on resisting systemic forces which can shape subtle and overt hegemonies within the institution.

### Transforming Pedagogical Frameworks

Never did I think I would make such an impact on the minds of students by showing and talking positively about BAME groups and referring to BAME authors who look like them. The room becomes more animated as previously quiet non-questioning BAME students' eyes widen with enthusiasm. There were nods of acknowledgement as I provided examples of black academic scholarship and critical analysis of the Eurocentric view of marginalised groups in British society. All students were intrigued by an alternative view a critique of the repetitious negative discourse and persistent pathologising of BAME groups. Students have commented on how positively refreshing, interactive and inclusive these seminars are.

Essentially, I provided a learning environment which allowed BAME students to *exhale*. This feeling of relief caused me to recollect my negative educational experiences. From secondary school the British education system has brought me moments of pain, anguish and instances of curiosity about whiteness. I thought it was just me being selfish wanting to learn about *my* history that connects me to something tangible, my being and my becoming. I was extremely disappointed and simply withdrew from anything Tudor, Victorian, Shakespearean not to mention WWI and WWII history. I struggled to relate to any of it, as I was excluded from these histories. It was only when I took control of my educational journey as an undergraduate, I felt I could learn alternative academic scholarship which made me feel included in society. To my realisation black scholarship was not new at all! Writings by black authors were always present but hidden almost like a latent form of knowledge never mine to embrace. My undergraduate degree provided a wide range of module options in year two. This was the greatest form of liberation for me, as I could finally loose the chains of core Westernised modules. At that moment, I was thirsty to know more about Caribbean literature, Black scholars the Pan-Africanist movement. These academics recognised and acknowledged my existence.

As a black female academic I relate to the issues of belonging and trying to engage and understand why BAME groups in society are where they are today — still displaced, experiencing moments of isolation and remaining marginalised in white spaces. From my perspective, the way BAME members of society are portrayed in the media and in mainstream society in general appear far too negative, sensationalised and extremely biased. I feel much more needs to be done in the university I represent, and it has made me more interested to know how BAME students are experiencing their curriculum. With my platform, I have an opportunity to do something that can gradually change misconceptions of minority groups.

I became more actively involved in order to challenge mainstream assumptions and be part of a social movement to decolonise the curriculum, through centering race within conversations about inclusivity and questioning the utilisation of reading material against the ever-growing diverse student demographic. Surely other academics are taking stock of this, but I find other academics carry on in the same fashion believing knowledge of the 'classic canons' of knowledge will be sufficient to enable students to gain a 'good degree'. It will be alright. Just deliver what you did last year. So business as usual. But it's not alright, apparently it never was. I believe we have a responsibility to teach in a holistic and inclusive manner with authentic global knowledge. This will provide an opportunity for cultural change in order to acknowledge the kaleidoscope of students of colour that have permanently transformed the makeup of the student population at this university.

It is evident that the tide is changing as the third generation of British born BAME students, international students and those from non-traditional routes into higher education begin to fill lecture theatres with a thirst for knowledge. These students must also be fairly represented within the curriculum and on reading lists. The effects and impact of BAME social movements of Rhodes Must Fall, Why is my curriculum white? and Why Isn't my professor black?[2] echo through the corridors of universities, creating critically conscious minds that question notions of whiteness.

Within institutions there exists uncritical and unexamined, unchallenged levels of whiteness in our pedagogical practices. Change for a more equitable and inclusive curriculum is imminent. I teach knowledge which originates from Western thought such as the Renaissance and Enlightenment periods which have been strategically disseminated to the academy during colonial and imperialist rule. This narrow knowledge and Eurocentric epistemic discourse taught in universities has become re-entrenched producing globalised inequality and Eurocentric learning practices with the notion of colour-blindness. It possesses the dynamics of 'imperialist amnesia' (Kapoor 2014). In this present day post racial and neo-liberal agendas prevail. They continue to support the white pillars and white walls of power in academia.

In the years I have spent teaching in higher education, attending Equality, Diversity and Inclusivity networks and projects, I have observed that change can move at an almost glacial pace because of where the power lies. The 'Decolonising' agenda needs to be understood as an intrinsically troubling process, one involving uncomfortable unsettling questions which disrupt entrenched ways of thinking and knowing. As an academic I listen and appreciate students' opinions and counter narratives coupled with changing perceptions of student's views about the way the topic on a module is framed and how and why it fits all too conveniently alongside normative whiteness and a dominant Eurocentric curricula. A research report by the Royal historical society stated many BAME respondents believe there are structural reasons for the absences of difficult and challenging histories such as Empire and decolonisation from school and university history curriculum. One BAME student argues that, 'White Britons need to be able to discuss uncomfortable histories without becoming defensive.'[3]

Numerous times, I have purposely and consciously included BAME examples, containing positive images in my teaching to negate deficit models that litter empirical research journals and core text of course modules which students accept as genuine. This is because if students (white or BAME) don't know the whole truth, they may remain unaware of positive BAME references within British society. Consequently, there is almost a hidden plethora of black intellectual thought of which few academics actively teach.

Over time, I have observed the effects of inaccurate knowledge transfer and this has resulted in BAME students being fearful of engaging with the concept of race and racism. A BAME student asked me if it was OK to speak about their experiences as they didn't want to come across as the black angry female mature student. I responded, 'on the contrary we value your unique experience others have yet to encounter.' She declared how grateful she was to know that she has a voice which is respected and legitimised. I have had several black students ask me if it was acceptable to discuss how they felt about being marginalised or misrepresented in society. I was disturbed by this sense of apprehension because students feared being reprimanded by white academics and would be marked down in their assignments if they were to present a critical view of white privilege within their social, economic and cultural lived experiences. Yet academics expect levels of critical analysis but not from a BAME perspective as this is not legitimised in the institution's production of knowledge. Surely this contributes to the so-called attainment gap as white students are praised for their originality of expression without fear of reprehension because there is no ambiguity within normative whiteness.

## Working in Partnership With Students and Staff Across Campuses

As the momentum builds on the eve the Diversify the Curriculum conference at the University of Kent's Canterbury campus, the reading list
review project at the Medway campus has also aroused interest from
staff and students. The two projects complement each other in terms
speaking for the same cause — to liberate the minds within the white
walls of higher education.

The conference reflects diverse student and faculty protests against
hegemonic neo-liberal practices and associated racialised class based
gendered inequalities within the institution and in particular within
the colonised curricula. The conference was committed to dismantling
dominant hegemony, hierarchies and concentrations of power and
control in the hands of the few. There was a counter-hegemonic approach
that unsettled and decentred the white canon of knowledge production.
Students displayed truthful and passionate dialogue which is hardly ever
offered in white spaces of learning. BAME students seemingly wore their
hearts on their sleeve, providing rich personal narratives about discrimination, white supremacy and white privilege inside the walls of higher
education.

The Decolonise the Curriculum panel consisted of a rich abundance
of experts and voices that provided an unprecedented and emotionally
charged discussion about white privilege, colour blindness and colonial
legacies. A critical race theory (Crenshaw et al. 1996) lens centred these
discussions, as students and esteemed speakers filled the room with
intellectual vigour. I am forever grateful to have witnessed and applaud.

From where I sit within the institution just seeing BAME academic
staff is not enough. I hold a deep sense of my own identity and positioning in the institution and am aware that how I portray myself to
BAME undergraduates is imperative to the decolonising the curriculum
movement. Being active and using my platform for positive representation is not hard to do but can be emotionally draining, as it is commonly
a commitment over and above the daily academic role. So why do I do
it? From my personal observations in higher education, BAME students
experience becoming a cultural jigsaw, constantly asking themselves
'where do I fit?' within this white space which is going to virtually be
their home for the next three or four years of their impressionable lives.
This is one of the many reasons why the themes of belonging and engagement hold a significant subjective and nuanced link with the so-called

BAME attainment gap and 'getting the best out of their degree' student experience' debate.

## Conclusion

As an academic, being part of this movement to Decolonise the Curriculum through pedagogic practices and dismantling the Eurocentric curricula through decentering whiteness has made me reflect through a critical race theory lens on my experiences. I believe there is still much to do towards stripping the white walls of academia (Decolonise the Curriculum manifesto).[4] The need for social justice in academia requires consistent collaboration, with students and staff as joint allies. As a sociologist with a keen interest in the application of critical race theory in education and aspirations for BAME families (Adewumi 2019), I have reflected on my role as a BAME female academic. I have begun to use my academic positioning which has created a conversation fusion of allies with Decolonise the Curriculum in the Kent Law School who are on another campus. This is again an unusual but timely achievement. Moving forward it is my intention to use this stage not to speak for those who are silenced by stereotypical projections and institutional structures which suppress their need to express how they really feel, but I further intend to use my academic status to create opportunities to support the making of a confident and vocal BAME student who questions the status quo and looks beyond the core reading during their time in a white academy.

I have come to recognise my own complicity whilst teaching the white canon and the knowledge of social science developed in Western Europe and North America. I found these to be filled with colonial bias intertwined in institutionally embedded bias of which it pains me to transfer to my students. I feel more empowered to contribute to change in my current place of work. This has required some levels of sacrifice including emotional and physical cost of going above and beyond which comes with being one of the very few BAME academics in my department on campus. You have this feeling in the pit of your stomach where you need to do more with your privileged position, having a platform I need to do this for BAME students as well as for my own children soon to embark on the journey into higher education. If you don't raise the issue to the surface with a heartfelt passion for change very few white academic counterparts will voluntarily lift their head above the parapet on issues of race than they would for class or gender. I offer my experiences of learning within the white spaces of educational institutions not to garner admiral comments such as 'look how far she's come, considering her background', but to emphasise when students are exposed to black academic authors, Pan-Africanist writings and postcolonial thought it can reignite confidence, repair damaged self-esteem and reconfirm educational aspirations. Armed with such rich diverse scholarship allows a student to further question the Eurocentric curricula experience with conviction and empirical foundation.

## Notes

1 The Kent Law School Decolonising the Curriculum Project (www.decolonise UKC.org).

2 https://www.theguardian.com/uk-news/2016/mar/16/the-real-meaning-of-rhodes-must-fall.

https://www.nus.org.uk/en/news/why-is-my-curriculum-white/.

http://www.dtmh.ucl.ac.uk/isnt-professor-black-reflections/.

3 https://royalhistsoc.org/racereport.

4 DtC Manifesto (www.decoloniseUKC.org/manifesto) at the University of Kent.

## References

Adewumi, B. (2019). Bridging the Gap: Using Bourdieu and Critical Race Theory to Understand the Importance of Black Middle-Class Parents' Educational Aspirations for Their Children. In: Starl, G., Wallace, D., Burke, C. and Threadgold, S. eds. *International Perspectives on Theorising Aspirations, Bloomsbury*, pp. 210–255.

Crenshaw, K., Gotanda, K., Peller, G. and Thomas, K. (1996). *Critical Race Theory: The Key Writings that Formed the Movement*. New York: New York Press.

Fanon, F. (2005). *The Wretched of the Earth*. New York: Grove Press.

Kapoor, I. (2014). Psychoanalysis and Development: Contributions, Examples, Limits. *Third World Quarterly* 35 (7), pp. 1120–143.

Rhodes Must Fall Oxford (2018). *Rhodes Must Fall: The Struggle to Decolonise the Racist Heart of Empire*. London: Zed Books.

Royal History of Society (2018). Race, Ethnicity & Equality in UK History: A Report and Resource for Change.

6

# Decolonising the University: A Movement that Must Look to History, and Remain Radical

*Dr Remi Joseph-Salisbury*
*Manchester University*

In recent years, we have seen a troubling resurgence of explicit national-ism, nativism, fascism, and racism. Whilst the lived experience of many Black and people of colour communities make clear that this racism is nothing-new (Brown-Vincent 2018), we would be complacent to overlook the lurch to the Right, and the mainstreaming of hate. As our communi-ties continue to battle with the devastating effects and affects of racism, it is important that we cultivate, nurture, and celebrate sources of hope.

Those of us looking for hope and inspiration would do well to look at the anti-racist student movements that have sprung up across UK university campuses over the last few years. Led by students of colour, these campaigns have taken aim at the dire state of our universities (Alexander and Arday 2015; Bhambra, Gebrial, and Nişancıoğlu 2018; Joseph-Salisbury 2019; Sian 2019). From the Goldsmiths Anti-Racist Action Occupation (Rawlinson 2019), to the smaller pockets of resistance across the country, student anti-racist action has coalesced into what now looks like a formidable movement with international impetus. Through campaigns like *Why is My Curriculum White?*, *Why Isn't My Professor Black?*, *I too am*, and *Rhodes Must Fall*, students are asking difficult questions of their institutions (Joseph-Salisbury 2018). The calls to decolonise are now reverberating around the hallowed halls of Britain's institutions. As the establishment backlash (and threat of co-optation) makes clear, this movement poses a real threat to the white supremacist underpinnings of our Higher Education institutions.

Any illusion that this is merely a bourgeoisie concern of privileged students fails to recognise precisely what is at stake. Higher Education plays a central and undeniable role in contemporary society. The role of higher education is not abstract, but inextricably tied to the production of knowledge, to the organisation of the labour market, to the qualifications of professionals, and — fundamentally — to the (re)production of white supremacy. Put another way, higher education is a key pillar of white supremacy. As an architect or structural engineer might worry, to attack a pillar is to threaten the whole structure. Whilst dismantling the system of white supremacy will require struggles beyond university campuses, students are taking seriously the importance of us each 'struggling where we are' (Hall cited by Gillborn 2008, p. 202). By taking on their institutions, students are creating a schism, and opening up possibilities to imagine something new.

Alongside students at a range of institutions, students of colour at the University of Kent have placed themselves at the centre of this struggle. Taking the fire to their institutions, these students — sometimes with the support of staff — are doing the work! Decolonise UoK has created a hub for radical thought and action. Nirmal Puwar (2004) argues that it is only through struggle and contestation that we glimpse problems that have thus far been normalised. Decolonise UoK has enabled us to see. As James Baldwin teaches, once we see, we must say that we know (Lester 1984). Once we know, we must act.

As Decolonise UoK makes clear, we can no longer tolerate a higher education system that feeds students a white curriculum: this is ontological and epistemological violence! Decolonise UoK's manifesto demands that we 'combat a narrow focus privileging the white canon' (p. 6). To decolonise is not to diversify: this work must go beyond reading lists, therefore, and engender a fundamental questioning of the ways in which we understand knowledge production. Universities must centre 'a diversity of perspectives, particularly from scholars of colour and from the global south' (p. 6). We cannot tolerate any longer, therefore, a professoriate that is overwhelmingly white, and contains so few Black women (Rollock 2019). We cannot tolerate the explicit and implicit interpersonal racisms that Black students and students of colour continue to face on campuses, and we must take the wellbeing of staff and students of colour seriously. As Decolonise UoK teach us, this is urgent. The student organisers at Kent have quite rightly highlight the extra burden that the weight of whiteness places upon them and students of colour at-large. They are quite right, then, to demand that universities make available 'race-literate' and 'culturally competent' support services.

Despite the disingenuous criticisms of the establishment, the Decolonise movement is not a whimsical endeavour. Students, at Kent and elsewhere, have taken seriously the importance of theory and study. This isn't a campaign built over night, but one that has been rigorously researched. At Kent, campaigners have sought the voices of students of colour, have liaised with staff, and have extended solidarity far and wide. To be successful, this must continue, and it must be strengthened.

This turn to history is imperative. Decolonise, as it is utilised in Higher Education, is at risk of becoming little more than a buzzword. Increasingly, 'decolonise' appears to stand-in for 'diversity', hollowed out of its radical potential, and co-opted by university establishment figures (Dar, Dy and Rodriguez 2018). In the face of this threat, historical analyses are essential. As Kwame Ture (2007, p. 185) put it: '[b]ecause revolutionary theories are based on historical analyses, one must study. One must understand one's history and one must make the correct historical analyses'. A look at the history of decolonial and anti-colonial movements shows that calls to decolonise should invoke something radical and uncompromising. Solutions cannot be piecemeal, but must shake the very foundations of our institutions. When the term is taken up by university establishment figures, then alarm bells should ring. To look at the history of decolonisation, is to see the shoulders on which we stand, and to know that 'decolonization is not a metaphor' (Tuck and Yang 2012).

To do any justice to anticolonial movements of the past, contemporary university decolonise movements must not limit their scope to curricula, but should question the dirty money that flows through our universities. To Decolonise is to condemn the support that our universities offer for racist institutions and for oppressive regimes.

A decolonial framework implores us to question, for example, the role of universities in training the police officers that harass and oppress black and brown communities across the UK. However, decolonial analyses do not stop here: they urge us to look beyond the parochialism of the UK. We might therefore ask why UK universities are involved in the 'training' of police in countries that have horrendous human rights records. What, too, of the entanglement of our universities in the development and trading of arms? This has to be intolerable. Similarly, the movement must not tolerate the ways that universities produce and enact (racialised) gentrification. Nor can it tolerate the underpayment and mistreatment of the most precarious of the university's workers — the cleaners and catering staff, for instance. To decolonise, will mean connecting with anti-racist movements outside of the university, to harness university resources for the 'wretched of the earth'. Reparations are long overdue!

The students leading these campaigns cannot do it alone, but they have created a context in which decolonisation of our institutions is imaginable and speak-able.

## References

Alexander, C. and Arday, J. eds (2015). *Aiming Higher: Race, Inequality and Diversity in the Academy.* London: Runnymede Trust.

Bhambra, G., Gebrial, D. and Nişancıoğlu, K. eds (2018). In: *Decolonising the University.* London: Pluto Press.

Brown-Vincent, L. (2018). Contextualizing Black Struggle in Trump's America, in Johnson, A., Joseph-Salisbury, R. and Kamunge, E. eds. *The Fire Now: Anti-Racist Scholarship in Times of Explicit Racial Violence.* London: Zed Books.

Dar, S., Dy, Angel M. and Rodriguez, J.K. (2018). Is Decolonizing the New Black? Sisters of Resistance. Available from: https://sistersofresistance.wordpress.com/2018/07/12/is-decolonizing-the-new-black/.

Gillborn, D. (2008). *Racism and Education: Coincidence or Conspiracy.* Abingdon: Routledge.

Joseph-Salisbury, R. (2018). Whiteness Characterises Higher Education Institutions — So Why Are We Surprised by Racism. *The Conversation,* 9 March.

Joseph-Salisbury, R. (2019). Institutionalised Whiteness, Racial Microaggressions and Black Bodies Out of Place in Higher Education, *Whiteness and Education,* 4(1), pp. 1–17, DOI: 10.1080/23793406.2019.1620629.

Lester, J. (1984). James Baldwin: Reflections of a Maverick. *New York Times* Book Review, 27 May. Available at: www.nytimes.com/books/98/03/29/specials/baldwinreflections.html.

Puwar, N. (2004). *Space Invaders: Race, Gender and Bodies Out of Place.* Oxford: Berg.

Rawlinson, K. (2019). Anti-Racism Activists End Goldsmiths Occupation, 29 July 2019. Available from: https://www.theguardian.com/education/2019/jul/29/anti-racism-activists-end-goldsmiths-occupation.

Rollock, N. (2019). Staying Power: The Career Experiences and Strategies of UK Black Female Professors, UCU. Available at: https://www.ucu.org.uk/media/10075/Staying-Power/pdf/UCU_Rollock_February_2019.pdf.

Sian, K. (2019). *Navigating Institutional Racism in British Universities.* London: Palgrave.

Tuck, Eve. and Yang, K. Wayne. 2012. Decolonization is not a Metaphor. *Decolonization: Indigeneity, Education & Society* 1(1), pp. 1–40.

Ture, K. (2007). *Stokely Speaks: From Black Power to Pan-Africanism.* Chicago: Chicago Review.

# 7

# Racialised Inequitable Exclusion and Educability: Reflections from a Black Professor

*Professor Lez Henry*
*University of West London*

I received an invitation from Dave S.P. Thomas to attend the Decolonise UKC student-led conference at the University of Kent in March 2019. I wasn't sure what to expect on the day, as often times student-led and student-centred fora, are marshalled by staff and as such, the freedom or courage to address the telling issues are limited. From the outset I realised this was clearly not the case here because the students began with an explanation of the importance and centrality of their voices to any conversation, regarding who is impacted the most by systemic and institutionalised racism. This set the scene for the ensuing discussion, both detailing and highlighting why it is crucial to the future of higher education that any thoughts universities may have on decolonisation cannot merely be a tokenistic, tick box exercise. Of equal importance their contributions highlighted the wider student experiences and not a myriad way and made known their crucial input and presence within the University of Kent's Decolonise the Curriculum initiative.

Additionally, I was impressed with the obvious staff-student collaboration that led to the creation of the Decolonise UKC Manifesto and the way in which it was presented by a team of students at the conference. This provided insight into the tangible change that students were seeking. Crucially, what was evidenced throughout was that the onus must be placed on institutions and faculty to effect positive, curricular change, because students' primary goal is to grow intellectually in an environment that is conducive to mutual learning. As such they cannot be expected to focus on their studies whilst championing/spearheading movements advocating for the necessary changes that were required in seeking what Robbie Shilliam calls 'epistemic justice'.

Consequently, the focus was on the introduction of complementary material that represents the contribution of Black, Asian and minority ethnic (BAME) communities to the storehouse of human knowledge which is not, as has been suggested within the wider public arena, a vulgar removal of the white middle class, male presence that currently dominates too many aspects of the way learning is experienced within higher education institutions. The obvious suggestion from the day was that by focusing on a more diverse and inclusive curriculum, all students will naturally benefit from more equitable outcomes based on skills and abilities and not be hindered by racialised forms of inequitable exclusion, that have little to do with the educability of BAME students.

§4

**POSTCOLONIAL BANTER**

# 8

# British Values

*Suhaiymah Manzoor-Khan*
*www.suhaiymah.com*

This chapter draws on the work performed at the launch of the DecoloniseUKC manifesto to rapturous applause:[1]

Young Muslims In Britain Often Straddle Two Worlds / They Appear to Have a Foot in Each Culture / Concerns Revealed Around the National Identification of Muslims In Britain / Review Raises Alarm Over Social Integration in The UK / Schools to Promote Fundamental British Values / The Face Of Britain Is Changing Beyond Recognition

I look in the mirror
it's not shattered, I am whole
no one foot in, one foot out
no reason I've got to learn *Britishness* from the somehow more devout
I'm not 'uneasy' 'torn' or 'straddling'
it's not shattered, I am whole
yet the opposite is somehow all that you'll get told
I mean I guess cos if it wasn't
if we faced up to the glass
you'd be left with the fact that I *am* inside I *am* Britain now, cos
Britain is bismillah
Britain is basmati rice
Britain is box braids and black barbers' shops, Bollywood and bhangra Britain
is Bradford and Barking and Birmingham
Britain is biriyani and black beans
Britain is black, Britain is brown
Britain is boys blasting dubstep on the bus to town
Britain is body-popping outside the tube
Britain is Brick Lane before it was cool
Britain is bilingual
Britain is the burka

Britain is praying in the changing rooms
Britain has its feet in your sink
Britain is bad at knowing itself, belligerent, and boring.
Britain has not *Changed Beyond Recognition* recognise it was never one thing
I am the inside you pretend is outside
but we have to stop pretending
Pretending the rolling hills are just romantic not remnants of injustices swept
under a rug like the tea didn't come from Asia
like its sugar wasn't grown by slaves
like dry humour isn't a way to just ridicule dissent
and queues don't expose the way we're always told to wait for change rather
than making it
and it's funny that over-apologising is seen as a national trait cos half of
history is still waiting

I look in the mirror
it's not shattered, I am whole
there is no 'brink' or 'turning point' I'm here.
Britain is barbaric
— oh sorry, did you think that was me?
Barbaric bystander straddling the boundary?
Not quite *inside* so you could say I'm the things you forgot like you're 'modern'
so I'm 'backwards'
you're 'democratic' so you say I'm not
when the truth is
Britain is blood on its hands and back-to-the-wall
Britain is selling weapons to the most repressive regimes in the world Britain
is the bombs the Saudis drop on Yemen
Britain is using fear to build surveillance apparatus since 9/11
Britain is believing in human rights whilst removing them all Britain is Yarl's
Wood, Brook House, Colnbrook and Morton Hall Britain is sixteen hundred
dead in or after police custody since 1990 Britain is no qualms about detaining
asylum seekers indefinitely
Britain is suicide attempts, secret courts and secret torture Britain is stopping
you at the border
Britain is Seeing it, Saying it, Sorting it — which means Britain is also
deporting it
cos what else do you do
when you look in the mirror and find
the sugar and tea had strings attached
the factories on the rolling hills depended on our labour the bombs destroyed
the homes of kids now at the border
Britain *is* barbaric

Britain is blindly patriotic
Britain is built on false narratives slices of other people's dishes
Britain is stolen artefacts in museums named after itself Britain is knife and
fork polite, stabbing you at will Britain is selective:
yours 'til its not; in yours 'til its not, then blaming you
Britain is borders
Britain is Brexit
Britain is spending on weddings but not fire-proofing homes
Britain is cutting mental health services yet somehow 'Strong & Stable'
Britain is 40% of young people in custody being from ethnic minority back-
grounds Britain is blaming them for this statistic, rather than asking difficult
questions
'cos
Britain is blaming the kids who aren't white Britain is blaming the Muslims
Britain is blaming the immigrants
Britain is blaming bureaucracy
Britain is not listening
Britain is Not That Great
Britain *is* breaking
but breaking everywhere except the place it points the finger because there's
only a few things left that are Great about Britain and they're that
Britain is bismillah, basmati and bilingual box braids and black barber's shops
Bollywood and bhangra
body-popping outside the tube
Brick Lane before it was cool
Britain is the burka
Britain is praying in the changing rooms Britain has its feet in your sink
Britain is your greatest nightmare
every repercussion you never thought through
Britain is the terror to be countered Britain is the mind to be got inside
I am the Great in Great Britain[2] now and aren't you terrified?

## Further Information on Specific Lines of the Poem

*Britain is the bombs the Saudis drop on Yemen* refers to the way BAE systems,
a British company that supplies arms, technology, planes and training to
Saudi Arabia is central to making Saudi Arabia's war in Yemen possible.
UK arms exports are leading to the murder of civilians in Yemen which
many have argued is a deliberate strategy — targeting civilians is illegal
under International Law. Where is Britain's 'rule of law' at play here?

*Britain is sixteen hundred dead in or after police custody since 1990* — since 1990 Inquest report that 1712 people have died in police custody or following contact with the police (June, 2019). 14% of those deaths were of BAME people, but BAME deaths occurred disproportionately due to use of force and restraint, showing the palpable racial dimensions of police violence.

Whilst we associate police violence with the USA and Black Lives Matter movement there, institutional racism in the UK police force also kills, 1712 is not an insignificant number. Is this the rule of law? Is this mutual respect?

*Yarl's Wood, Brook House, Colnbrook and Morton Hall* are four of eleven immigration detention/removal centres in the UK. Such centres are places where people who are seeking asylum (over 50%), 'undocumented' (without visas or paperwork mostly due to being refugees, trafficked or having experienced other violent conditions), and otherwise waiting to find out if the Home Office will grant them 'leave to remain' or deport them, are held. People can be held in these centres indefinitely — this means there is no maximum time limit on people's time in detention in the UK — it could be months or years — the UK is unique within Western Europe for this.

In 2017, over 27,000 people were held in immigration removal centres across the UK. Since 2000, at least thirty-nine people have died in UK detention centres (according to Inquest). Not only are detention centres effectively cages to hold and punish the most marginalised in, indefinite detention causes unbearable mental health problems due to the uncertainty and stress and there have been many reports of the physically and sexually abusive conditions in detention centres, too. Article 9 of the Universal Declaration of Human Rights says no one should be subject to 'arbitrary arrest, detention or exile', these centres clearly violate the principle of basic human rights ... Which British Value does this align with? Or are those values not afforded to you if the Home Office believe you don't have the right to be in the UK/don't have the right paperwork? For further information and follow the work/social medias of: SOAS Detainee Support, End Deportations and Detention Action

*Britain is secret courts and secret torture* refers to the fact that the 2013 Justice and Security Act introduced 'closed material procedures' meaning that the government can decide a case without giving any details or evidence to the defendant. All or part of a claim can be heard in closed proceedings that exclude even the claimant who is represented by a

'Special Advocate' who is not able to speak to the client once they have seen the 'sensitive material' of the case. Is this 'the rule of law' that is a central 'British Value'? For further information, read: Nisha Kapoor, Deport, Deprive, Extradite: Twenty-first Century State Extremism.

*Britain is deporting it* refers to the expulsion of people from the UK based on asylum claims being refused, visa/claims expired, or the Home Office deciding you are a danger to 'the public good'. The 'Windrush scandal' in 2018 when people (particularly British people from Caribbean countries who arrived in the UK before 1973) were detained, denied legal rights, threatened with deportation and deported (83 people) by the Home Office was a case of deportation that did not fit these already awful categories. Other deportation and extradition cases as well as removal of citizenship have also affected others through Counter Terror legislation.[3]

*Postcolonial Banter* (Verve Poetry Press, 2019) is Suhaiymah's debut collection. It features some of her most well-known and widely performed poems as well as some never-seen-before material. Her words are a disruption of comfort, a call to action, a redistribution of knowledge and an outpouring of dissent. Whilst enraged and devastated by the world she finds herself in, in many ways that world is also the normalised and everyday reality of her life. Hence, whilst political and complex in nature, her poetry is also just the reality of life for her and others like her. Life in a world where structural violence is rife makes it a shared knowledge, and sometimes, when possible, that shared knowledge is the subversive in-joke, the bonding glance of solidarity, or the passing nod of affection used by those who know it to survive those structures themselves. This collection is first and foremostly for them.

Ranging from critiquing racism, systemic Islamophobia, the function of the nation-state and rejecting secularist visions of identity, to reflecting on the difficulty of writing and penning responses to conversations she wishes she has had.

## Notes

1 https://www.youtube.com/watch?v=mg2L7TAR8j4&list=PLbAKlg2H-Hdu-v5ZPBMF6hta3PNe-aSob.

2 'British Values' are a set of four values introduced as part of the British government's Counter Terrorism strategy, particularly in schools. Promoting British values is therefore something that education providers are expected to do under the Prevent Duty which became a legal duty on public service providers

in 2015. The Duty connects teaching 'British Values' to 'preventing' young people being 'drawn into terrorism'. British values are defined as democracy, rule of law, individual liberty, and mutual respect and tolerance of different religions. To me this is very ironic since Britain has been one of the most violent and undemocratic nation-states in the world's history through its role in the trans-Atlantic slave trade, colonisation and imperialism, and direct and indirect involvement in wars and genocides. Through this poem I wanted to convey those ironies and show that the narrative Britain tries to promote to define its 'values' or 'itself' is really a project to define racial Others (people of colour and Muslims) as 'outsiders' to Britain. It is a way to deflect from and to not have to deal with the violence that the government and state create and perpetuate. It is a way to say 'we are not what they are, and what they are is whatever we say we are not'.

By defining Britain as democratic and tolerant, undemocratic tendencies and intolerance are displaced and scapegoated onto 'outsiders'. Subsequently 'Britishness' becomes a glorified imagining which in the end translates to nothing more than whiteness. I say this because the 'promotion of British values' relies on an assumption that they need to be taught to children from ethnic minority backgrounds (who are more associated with extremism and violence through measures like Prevent and structural racism), whereas government reports (e.g. The Casey Review, 2016) assume white children/areas with less 'ethnic minorities', are more likely to have 'British values' already. Since the whole concept is so clearly racialised (seen as something white people are born with and 'ethnic minorities' need to learn, develop and prove), and since no inherent or static 'British culture' has ever existed (Britain has never been geographically, ethnically, physically or ideologically one thing, cultures/nations never are), this poem tried to reveal the ironies of the charade and highlight that what Britain says it is contradicts what is actually does.

3  see more at: http://dde.org.uk/.

§5

# STRIPPING THE WHITE WALLS

# 9

# Podcast as Powerful Pedagogy

*Ahmed Memon, Joy Olugboyega (University of Kent)
and Dr Francesca Sobande (Cardiff University)*

## Introduction

This chapter provides reflections of the podcast series 'Stripping the White Walls' beginning with a reflection by Dr Francesca Sobande on podcast as a powerful tool for pedagogy.

The aims of this podcast were to create a safe space outside of formal environments to freely discuss our thoughts regarding the racialised issues that exist in higher education, then challenge them. Most importantly, the aim was to raise awareness of the racial disparities that exist within the academy so that we can effectively and (hopefully) permanently strip the *White Walls*. We are by no means experts, but young people who aim to educate ourselves and liberate our minds.

The name 'Stripping the White Walls' is a conscious and deliberate metaphor to address and reclaim the representation, voice and space for people of colour in the academy — both students and staff. The title signals the driving force of the podcast to tear down 'whiteness' as the only standard of knowledge and way of being. The podcast is meant to create principled, safe, collaborative space for students to discuss issues of race, gender and sexuality within higher education. Instead of having an 'expert' focus on academic knowledge, the podcast is a more conversational, experience focused discussion around these issues. The second part of the chapter 'decolonising a Fool's Utopia' reflects on a joint collaboration between the podcasts 'Fool's Utopia' with 'Stripping the White Walls'. It highlights how an otherwise 'expert academic knowledge' based podcast 'decolonised' itself in its form and substance through a conversation with 'Stripping the White Walls' where the focus was about experience as knowledge.

## The Pedagogical Power of Podcasts

The rise of social media and online content-sharing platforms has resulted in the increasing presence of different types of digital media in pedagogical settings. However, the role of podcasts is arguably rarely accounted for in scholarly work that focuses on pedagogical approaches; including accounts of pedagogical positions which are aligned with social justice activist principles. The strategies of #DecoloniseUKC have been varied and attuned to the many challenges faced by staff and students who experience racism and intersecting forms of structural oppression during their time at university. 'Stripping the White Walls' is one of the different ways that #DecoloniseUKC have shared their work.

The range of topics covered in the podcast include modern-day slavery, solidarity-building, the history of decolonial work, imperialism, colonialism, and why those involved in #DecoloniseUKC are striving towards challenging institutional white supremacy and colonialist structures across academia. The podcast is not a peripheral part of #DecoloniseUKC activity, it is one of several significant ways that those involved in such work have turned to digital processes and social media to ensure that their message can be accessed and understood by many. The institutionally racist and colonialist foundations of universities must be challenged. Now!

From Twitter to podcasts, #DecoloniseUKC has sought out ways to create and engage with digital content that will communicate their collective efforts, such as their manifesto which emphasises the need for more co-production between students and academics, as well as underscoring the importance of understanding and addressing experiences of oppression at the intersections of ableism and racism. Unlike lengthy and onerous academic publishing processes that sometimes solely result in output being inaccessibly stored behind a paywall, the process of producing a podcast provides a sense of agency and accessibility regarding how the work of #DecoloniseUKC is framed and communicated by those at the centre of it. In addition, the creation of a podcast can aid abilities to document and share thoughts and experiences concerning contemporary forms of racism at university, in a timely and relatively immediate way which can bring attention to issues as they unfold.

Identifying the potential benefits and pedagogical power of podcasts does not undermine the value of written scholarship. Rather, recognising the pedagogical power of podcasts is important for many reasons, including their capacity to reach a broad audience beyond the conventional exclusionary academic contexts. Still, it is equally as vital to acknowledge that podcast formats are not inherently accessible, nor are they specifically associated with anti-racist and decolonial collective organising. In fact, the continued proliferation of far-right and white supremacist podcasts highlights that the power of podcasts is often harnessed by people with radically different ideological positions, including individuals whose views are the antithesis of those at the root of #DecoloniseUKC efforts. For this reason, when reflecting on the pedagogical power of podcasts there is a need to reckon with their scope to both uphold and challenge racist perspectives.

Put simply, depending on the content of podcasts, who is producing them, and their intentions, podcasts can contribute to anti-racist and decolonial pedagogical pursuits, such as the student-led work of #DecoloniseUKC. Alternatively, they can be conduits through which people perpetuate hate speech and even incite violence. Thus, podcasts can be a rich source of consciousness-raising related to the colonial and institutionally racist legacy of higher education institutions. As podcast culture is typically more associated with popular culture than academia, its scope to contribute to pedagogical change may be dismissed by those most invested in maintaining the elitist status quo in higher education. However, it is precisely the fact that the production processes and content of podcasts can considerably differ to traditional academic output which presents the possibility of podcasts contributing to critical and resistant pedagogical approaches.

Through their podcast series 'Stripping the White Walls', #DecoloniseUKC students have recorded and shared conversations which address issues related to white privilege and working towards the development of curriculum content that is not simply Eurocentric in nature. As well as the podcast featuring discussions with the potential to provide people with a critical educational experience, accompanying content on the #DecoloniseUKC website includes references to resources that provide a good entry point for people's self-education and consciousness-raising regarding how institutional racism and colonialism functions in the academy. Therefore, it may be through engaging with the 'Stripping the White Walls' podcast that people find themselves further exploring and reflecting on literature and work which critiques the oppressive, racist and colonialist foundations of much of higher education.

Overall, the work of #DecoloniseUKC has involved the use of digital space and tools in ways that have raised awareness of related liberationist goals, in the words of those at the helm of such efforts. The podcast is but one of many examples of this and particularly demonstrates how the creation of digital media enable student-activists to bring attention to the challenges that they face and the reasons behind their collective-organising. Unfortunately, the digital visibility of such work can put individuals at risk. Targeted harassment, both online and offline, may result from increased visibility. Nevertheless, despite the dangers that can be involved in communicating #DecoloniseUKC activity through social media and podcasts, digital documentation and dissemination processes are crucial to critical interventions of those who intend to dismantle oppressive structures at the foundations of academia.

The production of podcasts such as 'Stripping the White Walls' can provide student-activists with the opportunity to foreground their perspectives and politics in a relatively autonomous way which does not require them to negotiate various potentially obstructive institutional gatekeepers. Moreover, by seeking out different creative channels through which to convey their message, #DecoloniseUKC have not simply spoken to or within their institution, they have reached out to many people and communities beyond it, and, ultimately, have refused to be confined by the walls of the academy.

# 10

# Stripping the White Walls: The Podcast

*Ahmed Memon and Joy Olugboyega*
*University of Kent*

So, what does 'Stripping the White Walls' mean? My initial thoughts
were to say 'knocking' instead of 'stripping' but as a collective, we didn't
want to come across as being too radical. I thought to myself that this
country is predominantly white and this isn't my 'home', so why don't
we just strip some white walls instead?

The purpose of stripping the white walls is not to remove and margin-
alise white history, but to expose the other ethnicities that were present
and contributed greatly to the development of the nation; to expose the
number of other 'colours' that have been concealed by whiteness. We
don't just exist on the door knobs or the frames, we also have our places
on these walls. Unfortunately, due to the inferiority and ignorance of a
large number of our white counterparts, they have felt the need to not
only ignore us but to completely erase the fact that we contributed to
what Britain is today.

The title of the podcast came from a recognition of the whiteness
of my educational institution and higher education across the UK in
general, where there is a lack of representation of people from ethnic
minority backgrounds. Since we are a part of the decolonising movement
across higher education, it made so much sense for me to suggest this
title for our podcast.

Before I go on any further, it is important for me to say that I believe
this movement begins with addressing the lack of representation, but
does not end there.

There are many ways that this title could be interpreted. For example,
the white walls represent the curriculum. Starting from primary school
all the way up to University, all that I saw was white history and white
individuals and when black history is brought up, it's almost always

about slavery, Martin Luther King, or Mary Seacole. The narrative of the 'white saviour' is constantly put forward. I believe this is as a result of colonisation. This may affect students that come from families without a contextual understanding of empire and colonisation (like myself) and teaching staff too. I often find that when European teachers are confronted by students that have this knowledge, they tend to feel threatened and become defensive.

The *White Walls* also represent the pedagogy and the staff (who are predominantly white, especially the further up the corporate ladder one looks). The ceilings that minority ethnic staff have to penetrate, unlike their white counterparts. This gives the illusion that in order to be successful or to be accepted that you have to attain whiteness. Fanons 'Black Skin White Masks' provides a brilliant example of this:

> When the black man comes into contact with the white world he goes through an experience of sensitization. His ego collapses. His self-esteem evaporates. He ceases to be a self-motivated person. The entire purpose of his behaviour is to emulate the white man, to become like him, and thus hope to be accepted as a man. (Sardar 2008, p. xiii)

Frantz Fanon, demonstrated how the colonised had unconsciously internalised their colonialism which may have resulted in a large amount of us individuals feeling somewhat inferior to our white counterparts and feeling that their behaviour was to be emulated in order to be successful.

Just like the colours of the LGBT flag are used to represent and reflect the diversity of the LGBT community the same effort should be applied when you see the kaleidoscope, when you see the manifesto and stripping white walls.

Stripping the White Walls also allows us to address and apply a critical race perspective[1] in analysing how whiteness works in the academy:

> The view that race, instead of being biologically grounded and natural, is socially constructed and that race, as a socially constructed concept, functions as a means to maintain the interests of the white population that constructed it.'[2]

The general idea behind our supporting podcast was to create an informal, unscripted and open space to share our thoughts and interview other academic activists who also have the desire to decolonise the curriculum and institution. The space was meant to be non-conforming and unhindered by curriculum or any kind of reading guide so the conversations could be led in an organic way with guests. This podcast was hosted by Ahmed, along with fellow students. We decided to team up, not only to bring forth our different perspectives and experiences, but to celebrate the fact that our common denominators are what brings us together; the fact that we are all ethnic minorities in the academy and have noticed the marginalisation and lack of representation of ourselves in the academy.

Although we are still in the early stages of this podcast — having recorded six episodes so far, which have discussed topics such as white privilege, Keynes College and its association with empire. We have also had the privilege of interviewing Professor Gurminder Bhambra (the first Professor of postcolonial and decolonial studies in the UK). Meeting Professor Bhambra made me realise how much of a privilege it was to have been in the same room as her and how important it was to see academics from ethnic minority backgrounds (especially women) in these spaces addressing these issues, while also highlighting the fact that Black and Asian academics are not anomalies and that they are not given the attention and credit that is owed to them.

### Decolonising a Fool's Utopia: Joint Episode With Stripping the White Walls

This particular section of the chapter is a reflection on the first recording of 'Stripping the White Walls' before its official launch. It was meant to be and was in fact, a deliberate collaboration between Stripping the White Walls and Fool's Utopia — a podcast on critical international law and international legal history.[3]

Fool's Utopia, is a podcast produced, hosted and planned entirely by Ahmed Memon and his colleagues at the Centre for Critical international Law and started in October 2018. The collaboration with Stripping the White Walls was meant to give support and facilitate the work of decolonising project at the University of Kent. The idea of the episode was for Stripping the White Walls to 'decolonise' a 'Fool's Utopia', in its form, substance and format.

Fool's Utopia is critical of traditional, European history and under-standing of international law, critical of our focus in the way we explore the subject is through the importance of colonial history, continuing forms of imperialism, race and gender within the subject of international law.[4] Our format and conversations often questions who count as an expert and the consequence of attributing legitimate knowledge only to certain people. We illuminate and interview critical legal scholars within the discipline. Nonetheless, our podcast remains a forum where the hierarchy of 'expertise' is maintained by centring voices that have 'academic' authority. The podcast Fool's Utopia, in its substance, was already involved with questions surrounding colonialism and imperialism in the making of international law. However, to do decolonial work is also to go beyond the substance and subvert a mode of producing knowledge in form as well. The format of the podcast Fool's Utopia was still bound by its colonial limitations — catering to and maintaining a hierarchy of knowledge producers — i.e. the academic 'experts.'

In order to decolonise a 'Fool's Utopia', it was important to think about what this meant in terms of the format, language and conversations in order to re-centre both the idea of what knowledge can look like, where it can come from and how it can be communicated. We realised that the biggest challenge of the podcast (a Fool's Utopia) has always been its inaccessibility to a broader audience beyond the academic sphere. This concern about inaccessibility is not just about language but also about politics of critical legal thinking. As Robert William Jr (1987) points out, critically approaching socio-legal issues is about politics which speaks to material realities of people and communities. Hence, 'rights' are more than just 'concepts' to be discussed by academics but real 'tangible experiences' of individuals and communities wrestling with inequalities. A podcast that centres decolonial work, itself, also, then needs to approached in a way where language is in fact inextricably linked to the politics of engagement with the people rather than about them or apart from them. This separation is at its root, colonial in nature, as it maintains a hierarchy of expertise coming from few privileged academics. Student centred podcasts, where the voices of the students emerge as knowledge producers, subvert this dynamic. This is even more relevant for a podcast that is based on racial injustice as students who deal with minoritisation and have experienced these issues need to be centred as knowledge producers.

In order to embody the spirit and purpose of the collaboration, it was important to speak to Joy, who was going to launch Stripping the White Walls, and has been part of the #DecoloniseUOK project. She introduced the project and outlined its relevance to the university environment and many concerns of students of colour. Having Joy in the podcast to talk about the objectives and work of the project, which has been rooted in experiences of students of colour in the University of Kent, was a particularly important way in which the episode itself progressed and differentiated from all our other 'Fool's Utopia' episodes. The language of the podcast was conversational rather than heavy in theoretical vocabulary. At the same time, our conversations around student experiences, their reliance on a white/European curriculum and reflections on what decolonisation meant to us made for a rich discussion, without the need for 'experts' as the source of this knowledge. Through our conversation we relied more on experiential knowledge that informs our understanding of the world. Further, outlining how when we do come across authors that speak to our experiences, we process that knowledge. Through this approach the podcast served as a pedagogical forum where students of colour, as Dolores Delgado Bernal (2002) observes, were centred as the 'holders and creators of knowledge'. A great example of this experiential knowledge was developed through interactions with scholarship we came across. This reflects how Joy and I shared what decolonisation meant for us and how we came to 'break the door of our awareness' about it. I shared how my understanding of generational violence on the psychology of post-colonial people became clear to me through the reading of how the British East India Company and British Empire's administrators embedded ideas of English modernity as a higher standard that different cultures of the Indian subcontinent needed to reach. Modernity, then in the everyday imagination of the postcolonial was understood as Anglocentric linguistic and cultural practices such as fluency of English and eating habits. To this day these are still held as standards of civilisation within post-colonial states but also more importantly in the psyches of people in the post-colony. As Joy mentions in the podcast itself, seeing black lives matter movement in the US but also in the UK was her encounter with conversations around issues of race along with reading about colonial history and literature beyond slavery and Martin Luther King. For example, in our conversation she expands on this and refers to reading J.A. Rogers' *From Superman to Man* (2014), the biography of Malcom X (2015) and Adam Hochschild's King Leopold's Ghost (1999) as being the books that shaped her initial interest and curiosity about history beyond what was being taught in schools. Reflecting on this scholarship for the both of us was not just an intellectual exercise but a reflection or echo of our own lived experiences. As Joy mentions, her experience of studying law was often one where she was left feeling isolated because she did not have any contact with anyone who could relate to her especially since the material she was studying did not make any allusions to race. What is key about engaging with course materials but also with the university experience is, as Joy mentions, empathy and not just sympathy. This was a sentiment that she said we could share but she knew her white peers or teaching staff would not. We shared, as I refer to it, a 'silent anger' in realising that we carried a sense of 'internalised inferiority' that has been passed down through generations. It is in the little ways of 'internalised inferiority' in our psyche we try to become 'better' and that better is always 'white European'. However, no matter how well we achieve those 'standards' — in our language, behaviour, 'education', we can never be or be accepted as good enough. This dissonance and 'internalised inferiority' is a generational trauma and violence that we come to face as we read, reflect on our experiences through learning. That learning, which can help us go through the process of 'breaking the door of our awareness' which inculcates a 'silent anger', 'pain' and yet gives us a new sense of consciousness. However, for the most part this is not given to us in university. As Joy says, it is only 'just, right, and responsible' that the university provides us with knowledge from other perspectives — not just white, European standards.

The podcast episode weaved in our personal stories as source of knowledge, in conversation with literature surrounding the history of decolonisation as it is told within the discipline of international law. As a podcast format and substance, it was conversational and reflection based where what we felt and experienced became a foundation of our reflection on anything academic. Looking back to the episode, what we were in effect doing was linking the personal, the local and the global, to say that decolonisation of the university is part of a much broader conversation. Within the bounds of this broader conversation 'decolonisation' is not just a moment — something that happened once upon a time — instead it refers to decolonisation as a 'doing'/ as a continuous struggle. As Joy points out, decolonisation is important because it reminds us that the struggle didn't stop and that words like 'diversify' do not pay attention to history and continuing struggles connected to our history. The word diversify, as Joy puts it, does not address the roots of the problem we face in the university specifically in relation to the BME attainment gap. Simply saying that 'diversifying the curriculum' is a solution ignores colonial history and its continuing legacy within our society which is reflected the experience of students of colour in universities.

Both Joy and Eric (podcast co-host) pointed out that even in a critical law school, whose hallmark is of deviating and questioning the norm, students of colour still feel a sense of alienation due to the content and environment in which they learn this content. I point out that the question then becomes who is this critical for and what is the focus of critical analysis. More often than not, critical legal thinking within the Law School when brought up 'provincialises critique developed by white/ European scholars', in the same way as Dipesh Chakraborty has argued that understanding of history is provincialised to Europe (Chakraborty 2008). This is an important point we reflect on during this podcast when talking about post-colonial scholarship. Taking Hamid Dabashi's position on this, I point out that even when one speaks of decolonial scholars their conversations are often related to and centred around white/European philosophy instead of understanding scholars of the global south on their own terms and context (Dabashi 2015). Eric Leofledd, my colleague and co-host of the podcast Fool's Utopia, points out how this tendency to refer to and claim ownership of scholars like Fanon, stems from a need to re-centre conversations on European scholarship to 'redeem' themselves of their colonial past — i.e. it is a response of white guilt followed by white saviour complex.

Towards the end of the podcast episode and throughout we kept referring to the idea of 'stopping and listening, looking back and thinking' to focus on what has been going on throughout history and continues to happen. This episode was a deeply personal one, as it should have been, but also one where we — especially Joy and I — thought about what it meant for us to stop, listen and reflect. At the same time, when confronted with the question of where does the struggle lead to and if there is an end, Joy stated that 'decolonisation' will always be the continuous struggle. To see its end is to miss the point of it as the act of 'doing', rather than an end in and of itself. In writing this particular section of the chapter, I found myself reflecting once more and remembering that perhaps the ethic of decolonisation in all its modes must be in continuing to stop, listen, look back and think about our responsibility. In doing so, I realised that the podcast format as a pedagogical tool needs to be and has to be inherently decolonial in nature not just in its substance but also its format, language and reflections that can subvert power hierarchies around who produces and holds knowledge. Thus, even if, as Joy observes in her section within this volume on 'Stripping the White Walls', we are by no means experts. For me, this conversation was one that was far more valuable than 'expert' knowledge. It was about experiential knowledge, empathy, community and reclaiming our voices through the podcast.

## Notes

1 This was first used as an analytical framework to assess inequity in education.

2 Curry, T. (2019). Critical Race Theory, Social Sciences. [online] *Encyclopaedia Britannica.* Available at: https://www.britannica.com/topic/critical-race-theory.

3 'Fool's Utopia', https://soundcloud.com/user-919369831.

4 The podcast is influenced in its approach to international law and its history from Third World Approaches to International Law frameworks, see specifically Antony Anghie (2007).

## References

Anghie, A. (2007). *Imperialism, Sovereignty and the Making of International Law,* 37. Cambridge University Press.

Bernal, D.D. (2002). Critical Race Theory, Latino Critical Theory, and Critical Raced-Gendered Epistemologies: Recognizing Students of Color as Holders and Creators of Knowledge. *Qualitative Inquiry* 8(1), p. 105.

Chakrabarty, D (2008). *Provincializing Europe: Postcolonial Thought and Historical Difference.* Princeton NJ: Princeton University Press.

Dabashi, H. (2015). *Can Non-Europeans Think?* London: Zed Books Ltd.

Hochschild, A. (1999). *King Leopold's Ghost: A Story of Greed, Terror, and Heroism in Colonial Africa.* Houghton Mifflin Harcourt.

Rogers, J.A. (2014). *From 'Superman' to Man.* Middleton CT: Wesleyan University Press.

Sardar, Z. (2008). Foreword to the 2008 Edition, in Fanon, F. (1964/2008) *Black Skins, White Masks.* London: Pluto Press.

Williams Jr, R.A. (1987). Taking Rights Aggressively: The Perils and Promise of Critical Legal Theory for Peoples of Color. *Law & Ineq.* 5, p. 103.

X, Malcolm (2015). *The Autobiography of Malcolm X.* Ballantine Books.

§6

# TALKING INTERSECTIONALLY
# WITH CHANGE AGENTS

# 11

# The Elephant in the Room: Conversations with Muslim Women

*Wahida Ahmed*
*University of Kent*

## Introduction

Having lived in one of the most diverse cities on earth (London) my whole life, moving to Canterbury to attain a degree in Religious Studies, was a culture shock that I was not prepared for.

In February 2015, just after the Charlie Hebdo shootings, I came to Canterbury for the first time with my mother, grandmother and aunt to house hunt and for a day out down South. Although I would normally wear the *abaya* (religious gown worn by female Muslims), on this day I decided to wear 'normal' Western clothes as I was aware of the rise of Islamophobic attacks around this time. My attempt to 'normalise' the appearance of my family failed. Little did we know that our day trip to Canterbury would be remembered for being one of the most vilifying days of our lives. Without going into too much detail, this day proved to us that truly actions speak louder than words. Although few people vocalised this, the message was clear; that we were not welcome and that we should '*go back to where we came from*.' I would like to clarify that this is where I come from: Britain is where I come from.

However, it is times like this that put me and many other BAME citizens in an identity crisis. This crisis is something that I only experienced after moving out of London and it messed with me so much that my entire university life became less exciting and more miserable. There are many such stories and many such voices that are forced to be silenced because of fear of safety, because freedom of expression is a myth to most BAME citizens, because BAME citizens do fear jeopardising their education and career, and really because BAME citizens have not been fortunate enough to have a space to open up about these things. Therefore, when I was approached to help lead a project like this (the Decolonise UoK project), that would help give BAME students the freedom which everyone else other than ourselves enjoy, I could not back away.

I was given the task to lead two focus groups with Muslim female students so that they could share their experiences. Strangely enough, although I have had numerous conversations of the like, many feared signing up even though they were assured anonymity. They feared that disclosing their experiences would aggravate the issue, something I used to feel too. Racism and religious discrimination are like recurrent cancers. It will not go away by ignoring; it needs constant treatment. Like this, the ills of society is in need of constant treatment and the only way to do this is by creating awareness to address it rather than cover it. Although the idea of curing racism and prejudices like these is contested, it is without a doubt something society should work towards.

My focus group co-leader and I chose to lead the focus groups to contribute to the research. I will be using data from the focus groups to discuss various instances of racism faced by BAME students in my university, with a particular focus on the female experience of Islamophobia. I hope you find this enlightening and I hope I can convince you to join us in our fight to eradicate institutional racism, and make Britain truly a nation of equality.

### Racism and Islamophobia/Anti-Muslim Racism in the Classroom

This section begins by defining racism and Islamophobia, particularly emphasising that Islamophobia is a form of racism too. According to the Oxford Dictionary, racism is 'prejudice, discrimination, or antagonism directed against someone of a different race based on the belief that one's own race is superior.' Islamophobia (although 'anti-Muslim racism' seems more suitable) is commonly used to describe discrimination or hostility towards Muslims and Islam. This description may be disputed but I am simply describing it in the context which it is used by most of society today. Islamophobia falls under the category of 'non-colour coded racism' as described by Lavalette and Penketh.

> The victims of racism may be black and Asian men or women, or they could be Polish or Romanian workers, or people from Rom Afro-Caribbean Society a communities or perhaps, most demonised of all, people from

Muslim communities from anywhere across the globe. (Lavalette and Penketh 2013, p. 34)

Time and time again, the focus group participants explained that 'the general popular discourse against Islam ensures that the British Muslim community as a whole is stigmatised for the actions of a few' (Lavalette and Penketh 2013, p. 43).

I have overcome some of the obstacles I faced due to prejudices within the institution and now hold a First-Class Honours Degree. Up until the final term of my final year of university, I was constantly questioned by people, young and old, about my choice of course. 'You do religion, you study philosophy? Do you just do Islam? Are you allowed to?' To answer those irrational questions, I mention that I actually focused on government and religion, sociology, anthropology and psychology of religion, as well as philosophy of world religions and non-religion.

Throughout my first year, I chose to wear the *abaya* as I had been for many years. Very few people in my classes would talk to me unless they had to, as thought I was something to be feared. From my second year onwards, I essentially decided to conduct a social experiment; I was so alienated and made to feel incredibly uncomfortable that I felt the need to wear 'normal' Western clothes while at university. From then on, people were much warmer towards me. However, whenever I would go back to London, I would go back to wearing my choice of religious clothing, without the fear of prejudices.

One of my most shocking experiences has been when the topic of 'ethnic minorities' would come up in certain modules; the only people that attended those lectures and seminars were in fact the hand full of ethnic minorities out of at least forty other white students. This is the society we live in. And this is the so-called 'university experience' that I had. Racism and Islamophobia in the classroom are so discrete, that it is not always proven by our research. Despite this, ninety six percent (96%) of the students in our focus group said that they have experienced some form of racism, be it on part of fellow students, tutors or even the department/school.

The right to freedom of expression has been so misconstrued that it supposedly allows the freedom to discriminate. In the name of freedom of expression, extreme right-wing rhetoric views are expressed in the university, mobilising racist and Islamophobic ideologies, but when ideas of equality and inclusivity are pushed, it takes a long time to implement what should be considered basic human principles. The students who participated in my focus group explained that they felt like they could not exercise their freedom of speech due to discernible prejudices that curtails their ability to speak and write freely; this hinders their educational journey. This restriction has gone so far that a participant recalled a time when as a politics student, they were accosted in the library by a white student, who asked, 'are those your books?' The books were on terrorism, as she was researching and writing on terrorism. This worried her and so she changed her topic. I have constantly written to please the examiner, to get that first, but this was unacceptable. Universities are supposed to be a platform where we should be able to write freely, but clearly that freedom is not given to BAME students as of yet.

Freedom of expression has long been exploited to advocate racism and religious intolerance, to the extent that focus group participants said that they felt threatened by racist and anti-Muslim racist societies across the campus. They said the local mosque has been attacked at times, and what was really interesting is that in that particular instance, the university had no prayer room on campus be it for Muslims or a multi-faith prayer room. When students made requests they were denied this space and told to use the local mosque and make it appear as though the mosque belongs to the university. But when the mosque and the local Muslim community are attacked, the university conveniently takes a back seat and hushes itself.

As *'racially minoritised'* — not minority as we are not minor nor a minority considering the statistics — students, focus group participants expressed on several occasions, that they had been made to constantly represent Islam and their ethnic background.

> I am one person. I am a Muslim, not Islam. I am Asian, not Asia. I am black, not Africa or the Caribbean. (Focus group participant)

Throughout my degree, I have not only been used as a representative but also been given the responsibility — yet this has been portrayed as something I have been bestowed with and should feel privileged about — to essentially fix the school's flaws. I have been an opportunity for the institution to tick boxes, so that they may say that there was a BAME, female, Muslim, First-Class student in the department who actively sought to make change and that they took it on board. It is amusing to think that recognising me as the first Muslim Asian female for contributing the way I have at the end of my degree with a voucher, is considered an achievement on the part of my school. I am not interested in tokenism. No longer will my hard-work be used to paint an illusory pretty picture. I did not attend university to be a cultural and religious negotiator. No one has done me any favours by *honouring me as the first of my kind* to do this kind of work, I do not owe anyone, I was not given my First-Class Honours Degree, I EARNED IT, just like all my other BAME peers. This excerpt is an accurate reflection of my experience at university:

> I began my graduate work in a white, male-dominated department with little access to diverse voices (women, minority or indigenous scholarship). I learnt about the colonial structures of education through my own volition. It was double-work to learn in this way because I still had to understand the dominant discourses in my field of study. I took it upon myself to read beyond my area into feminist theory, anti-oppression, anti-racism, whiteness studies, as well as exploring the experiences of minoritised educators and administrators. Learning what is not taught requires effort but that is one way to move past the limitations of the colonial, patriarchal, Eurocentric constructions of higher education. You can't simply fall back on expecting minoritised students to fill in curricular gaps for you (and all your students). Their job is to learn, not teach. If you want them to teach, then you need to remunerate them for their contributions. Otherwise they carry a burden of responsibility that is unequally applied in the classroom and they are even more marginalised and can face victimisation when the knowledge and experience they share is resented by classmates (and sometimes by instructors too).

Too many of us are repeating the same journey at universities now. My focus group participants expressed how weighed-down they feel with this burden on their shoulders. It is now time for those professionals hired by institutions to do their own work, and if this is now at an area of their expertise, then they should acknowledge that and appoint ethnic scholars, scholars of decolonial studies, as we are not the first to work on this and not going to be the last.

**Prevent: What Is It Preventing?**

Prevent awareness training provides a scenario concerning a Muslim school girl who replaces her Western dress and socialising activities, with wearing a hijab and taking a keen interest in Islam. This change in appearance/behaviour is framed as an early warning that she could go on to potentially engage within extremist activity (Sian 2017).

For anyone that wishes to deny the existence of anti-Muslim racism, I question their awareness. Islamophobia/anti-Muslim racism does exist at an institutional level. Why else has the *niqab* (face veil) has been banned in France and Belgium? Why else is there a ban on minarets in mosques in Sweden? Why else are there discussions in the UK of banning students in schools from wearing the hijab or fasting in Ramadan? Why else has the UK structured one of the most advanced legal systems known as Prevent, putting Muslims under even deeper surveillance than the rest of society?

Prevent is one of four programmes under the government's counter-terrorism strategy. According to Prevent:

> Radicalisation' refers to the process by which a person comes to support terrorism and extremist ideologies associated with terrorist groups (HM Government 2015, p. 21). However, 'the current understanding of "radical" has become synonymous with fundamentalism, extremism, terrorism, Al-Qaeda, Islamism, and is loosely applied in conjunction with Islam.' (Elshimi 2017, p. 21)

Prevent's focus shifted from 'radicalisation' to 'de-radicalisation' in 2011 (Elshimi 2017, p. 2). Prevent assumes that Muslims are most at risk of being radicalised; this assumption has led to the alienation of Muslims, making them targets rather than citizens of Britain. Prevent has been under indictment of 'spying' and 'gathering intelligence' on innocent Muslims in various articles (HC 2010, 11–13). Witnesses found that 'Prevent has too strong a focus on Muslims and insufficient regard to other forms of extremism, such as that stemming from Far-Right politics' (HC 2010, p. 20). Prevent also contributes to widening the schism of 'them' and 'us', as it has only served to segregate rather than unite British Muslims with the rest of society. An issue with 'de-radicalisation' is that it suspects one of a crime not committed. 'UK de-radicalisation targets individuals who have not necessarily engaged in violence, who may not even have links to wider terrorist networks' (Elshimi 2017, p. 5). The House of Commons (HC) highlights 'Prevent "criminalises" Muslims by labelling them all as being at risk from violent extremism' (HC 2010, p. 9). This is precisely what happened with one of our focus group participants.

As a student who has been in higher education, I have not only been trained to identify 'potential indicators of extremism' but have also been affected by the implementation of the Prevent strategies myself. An instance shared by a research participant shows how deeply 'concerned' institutions have become regarding the lives of Muslims. She told me how throughout school she did not wear the hijab and generally dress more modestly and chose to wear regular western clothes, but when she moved on to sixth form, she decided to wear the hijab and just a more modest dress code, but still Western. But from that first day at sixth form, she came under the radar of the school senior management team and local authority. When one of her teachers pulled her up to have a meeting, which in fact turned out to be an assessment to check for radicalisation, she said:

> I did kind of feel attacked because I thought they knew me and I knew them as I've been at the same school since year seven, but I guess not. (Focus group participant)

She said that she was aware that this particular region has seen a few instances of radicalisation and so she cooperated, but also, she did not really have a choice. What was most distressing was the depth and length of her surveillance. What should have been a time to enjoy sixth form with friends, completing A-levels and preparing for university became a nightmare of harassment simply because she chose to practice her religion.

Human rights is an interesting topic itself. 'There has always been multiple levels of colonisation in the story of human rights' (Shetty 2018). Human rights have worked to promote women's rights and LGBTI rights, yet we have also seen the 'appropriation and domination of human rights by Western powers, often for neo-colonialist projects' (Shetty 2018). But the 'Western hypocrisy around rights found its absurd apotheosis in Guantánamo Bay — a human rights vacuum created explicitly in the service of a 'war on terror' being fought in the name of freedom, and the values underpinning human rights. This is where it all unravels. And we see further evidence of that hypocrisy and selectiveness today in the brazen violation of the rights of refugees, and rampant Islamophobia' (Shetty 2018). It just really gets me thinking, it is remarkable how one's appearance and choice of clothing can define them and how many various interpretations there are. No one stops to ask the individuals themselves their definition. Instead, a young black male in a hoody is problematic; a woman in a hijab and/or abaya and niqab is problematic. Yet, for centuries now, university graduation ceremonies, namely the dress-code, are rooted in Islamic history. It is not a problem to wear the black gown and cap, which is an ancient Islamic tradition as students would wear their robe and hold the Qur'an above their head, with the tassel being the bookmark, upon completion of their Islamic studies qualification (Zain 2013). It certainly does not appear to be a problem to bury these histories. But why are we burying that which continues to live?

Returning to the title of this section, PREVENT, what is it preventing? Any claim that it is preventing radicalisation and extremism is false. In fact, it may be said that the scheme has been counter-productive as the exasperation and isolation PREVENT has caused may even be leading Muslims to becoming vulnerable.

### Gendered Islamophobia: The Problem of the Hijab

> Whenever the topic of Islam came up in class, I'm so cautious that I would avoid talking, even though everyone is looking to me for a response, because I am learning too, so I hate it when I am expected to just know. Based on my hijab, they have decided what they want to hear. I am not in that lecture to defend Islam, I will use other appropriate spaces for that, but it's more because I don't want to be their source of knowledge for Islam because I am still learning myself, I am no scholar. (Focus group participant)

According to Tell Mama, a project that records Islamophobic attacks, there was a 700% increase in the number of anti-Muslim hate crimes in 2017 post the Manchester Arena attack (House of Lords 2018, p. 5). According to the House of Lords, 'most victims were female (57.5%), most perpetrators were male (64.6%). A clear majority (72%) of the perpetrators were white men' (House of Lords 2018, p. 4). Women still seem to be an easy target, and the hijab has caused women to be even more susceptible to these attacks. Research participants have disclosed them being spat on at their hijab, but there were more reports of verbal abuse. This is unacceptable. But what is being done to stop this? And in fact, it is not just Muslim women, African and Sikh women who cover their hair have been mistaken for Muslims and as a result have experienced abuse. This was also detailed in the focus group where a student said,

> it's also so annoying that no one ever wants to sit next to me or make friends, but when it comes to seminar discussions or group work, because I am the only one who has done all the reading, they then want to talk to me. Besides that, I don't want to talk because I don't want to give them

that satisfaction, because they're not even going to listen to what I have to say, they just see what is on my head. (Focus group participant)

Notions of the hijab being associated with oppression or conservative ideology continue to lurk around society and campuses. Some participants felt that they felt somewhat safer on campus then outside of it with their hijabs, particularly as the region (Canterbury) is not so diverse. Others have experienced attacks, both verbal and physical. According to a National Union of Students (NUS) study, one in three respondents feared being attacked because they are Muslim, with Muslim women being more worried due to their choice of wearing Islamic clothing. One in three respondents had experienced some form of anti-Muslim racism (NUS, 2018, pp. 8–9). One night on campus, while walking to my accommodation, I was sworn at by a few boys and asked horrendous questions, such as, 'what's underneath all that?' How does one respond to that? Other cases involve white men and women alike telling Muslim women to stop wearing the hijab as we are apparently being oppressed and encouraging oppression by endorsing the hijab. I do not recall telling you that I am being oppressed. We are not in need of saviours, rather we would appreciate you being our allies.

**Intersectional Feminism**

I grappled with the idea of calling this section 'the myth of intersectional feminism ... ' as the kind of feminism recognised and supported by most of society is white feminism, feminism that recognises white women's problems, — something which a lady kindly shared of how difficult it was for her to make it to the esteemed position she is in now, at a conference seeking to decolonise the curriculum — feminism that seeks equality for white women, feminism that celebrates what the suffragettes and suffragists did in the late nineteenth century. Although there are some movements that discuss intersectional feminism, there is not nearly enough recognition of BAME women's issues, of the rights BAME have had for centuries before women in the West did. It is high time that BAME women receive the same rights. It is shameful to think that rights are considered a luxury for BAME women.

According to the most recent report released by the House of Commons, the UK unemployment rate for white citizens was 3.4% while it was 6.9% for BAME people (Powell 2019, p. 1). 'The unemployment rate was highest for people from a Bangladeshi background (13%), followed by those from a Pakistani or Black background (9%)' (Powell 2019, p. 2). But it is worse for BAME women with the highest unemployment rate among Pakistani or Bangladeshi women at 14%, in contrast to 4% of overall female unemployment (Powell 2019, p. 3). For too long these statistics have defined us as incapable, little has been done to reduce these statistics as the structures preventing us are still stable.

**Ethnic and/or Religious Societies: The Only Safe-Haven for BAME Students on Campus**

When the focus group participants were asked about 'belonging', there was almost a unanimous energy expressing that belonging is foreign at university for BAME and Muslim students.

> You never really feel like you belong, just over time you get used to the place and learn to get comfortable and make peace with the situation for your own well being. (Focus group participant)

Considering that 'creating a sense of belonging' is a key value in UK Higher Education, some institutions have done little to help feel BAME students as though they belong. There is always some form of isolation and alienation felt by BAME students. Freshers week is supposed to be the time for students to settle into university so that they can start to feel a sense of belonging, but this is unheard of when it comes to Muslim students in particular. Many of my research participants felt that they struggled to make friends in fresher's week as people form their friendship circles from activities that completely disregard the Muslim student population. According to the participants as well as in my own experience, fresher's week events and societies constantly revolve around alcohol-based events, shutting a whole group of people who may not even be Muslim, but may simply choose to abstain from alcohol. Even sports societies have various initiation tasks that many would deem inappropriate, such as, running around on a field unclothed. The participant continued saying,

> but if it wasn't for ISOC and the Mosque, I don't think I could have stayed here, it really helped me get through university, especially when you're so far away from home. It's the only place where you can meet people with the same value. (Focus group participant)

Why is it still the case that at universities, ethnic and/or religious societies, are the only safe haven for BAME students? Why is it that the Islamic Society or African-Caribbean Society are the only places that BAME students feel welcome? Is it because you would typically find people of a similar background here, or is it because other societies are innately white and exclusivist? Rigorous reform is needed if 'belonging' is something that universities want to continue to brag about.

## Conclusion

> There are many similarities between how students experience colonial classroom practices and how these manifest in university meeting practices. In both scenarios those who can speak are those who already have the currency to do so. Others, concerned about how their accents, use of language and lived experiences will be judged, remain silent and left out. (Behari-Leak et al. 2017)

Racism and Islamophobia continue to segregate society and hatred is deeply embedded in the colonial structures that still exist. They evidently deprive the BAME community from equality through the prejudices across the board, be it in education, employment, social services, and so on, from birth till death. The labelling of Muslims as a 'suspect community' under the PREVENT scheme (O'Toole et al. 2015, p. 163) has disrupted the livelihoods and education of Muslims in Britain. Islamophobia is one of the most rampant forms of racism in the West, and women face the brunt of it.

The term 'unconscious bias' is a common phrase used to describe supposedly unintentional racism. Institutions, including universities, use it so prevalently, particularly in 'diversity' and 'equality' training programmes, that the level of arrogance and self-forgiving nature as an effort to maintain white innocence, though should not, still surprises me. To claim that racism can be unconscious suggests that is so deeply embedded that it is impervious to change; it naturalises it; it makes it appear as something biological when in fact racism is a man-made social construct. It denies racism. This is another demonstration of preserving white superiority, a way to avoid ownership, to deny fault. When filling in forms, height or weight is not asked about, but 'ethnicity' is. Ethnicity is simply a revised method of racial thinking. The concept of ethnicity is rather complex, and to say that it is unconscious is implausible.

Diversification is not sufficient in the battle against institutional racism, rather there is need for a thorough decolonisation process to tackle deeply embedded prejudices (Bhambra et al. 2018, p. 7). Decolonisation is not just about diversification, rather it is an effort to reveal the ideology of white superiority that lies within the structures through which our agency is restrained. Decolonisation is an effort to remove all the hinderances faced by the BAME community due to the preservation of colonial mentality. And this should not be a movement limited to BAME students, rather something that all of humanity should strive towards. Only then can we truly boast about equality, for some façade about multiculturalism does not equate to equality. 'Multiculturalism helped create new divisions and more intractable conflicts which made for a less openly racist but a more insidiously tribal Britain.' (Malik 2009, p. 54) The Racial and Religious Hatred Act 2006, which may be considered the replacement of blasphemy laws, has done little to protect religious and ethnic minorities. In fact, Brexit results reflect precisely how divided Britain is, and racism and Islamophobia are so deeply embedded in our minds and institutions that it seems that our journey to decolonise will be arduous but worthwhile.

Decolonisation is an open invitation, rather than invasion of BAME livelihoods, to break down colonial structures. I request not only BAME students and professionals alike to use the platforms that they have access to, to begin to decolonise their spaces and institutions, but also ask our fellow white citizens to study and teach colonial history accurately and increase awareness and become allies in our fight for equality.

## References

Behari-Leak, K., Masehela, L., Marhaya, L., Tjabane, M. and Merckel, N. (2017). Decolonising the Curriculum: It's in the Detail, Not Just in the Definition. *The Conversation*. Available at: https://theconversation.com/decolonising-the-curriculum-its-in-the-detail-not-just-in-the-definition-73772.

Bhambra, G., Gebrial, D. and Nişancıoğlu, K. (2018). *Decolonizing the University*. London: Pluto Press.

Elshimi, M. (2017). *De-radicalisation in the UK Prevent Strategy*. 1st ed. Oxford: Routledge.

*Further Education Participation* (2019). [Online]. Available at: https://www.ethnicity-facts-figures.service.gov.uk/education-skills-and-training/

apprenticeships-further-and-higher-education/further-education-participation/latest.

HM Government (2015). *Prevent Document*. Crown copyright.

House of Commons (2010). 'Prevent and Contest' in *Preventing Violent Extremism*. London: The Stationery Office.

House of Lords (2018). *Islamophobia In The UK Debate On 20 December 2018*. London: House of Lords Library.

Lavalette, M. and Penketh, L. (2013). *Race, Racism and Social Work*. Bristol: Policy Press.

Malik, K. (2009). *From Fatwa To Jihad: How The World Changed: The Satanic Verses To Charlie Hebdo*. London: Atlantic Books.

McGregor, R. and Park, M. (2019). Towards a Deconstructed Curriculum: Rethinking Higher Education in the Global North. *Teaching in Higher Education* [Online] 24:332–345. Available at: https://www-tandfonline-com.chain.kent.ac.uk/doi/full/10.1080/13562517.2019.1566221.

O'Toole, T., Meer, N., DeHanas, D., Jones, S. and Modood, T. (2015). Governing Through Prevent? Regulation and Contested Practice in State-Muslim Engagement. *Sociology* [Online] 50(1), pp. 160–177. Available from: http://journals.sagepub.com/doi/pdf/10.1177/0038038514564437.

Sian, K. (2017). Born Radicals? Prevent, Positivism, and 'Race-Thinking'. *Palgrave Communications* [Online] 3. Available at: https://www.nature.com/articles/s41599-017-0009-0.

Tate, S. and Page, D. (2018). Whiteliness and Institutional Racism: Hiding Behind (Un)Conscious Bias. *Ethics and Education* [Online] 13:141–155. Available at: https://www.tandfonline.com/doi/abs/10.1080/17449642.2018.1428718.

Zain, A. (2013). Historical Origin Of The University Gowns And Mortarboards. [video]. Available at: https://www.youtube.com/watch?v=Bb21j1IIu2w.

# 12

# Race, Religion and the Male Experience: Intersectional Conversations with Muslim Men

*Ahmed Memon*
*University of Kent*

My own position is as a Muslim PhD student who is being trained in 'critical' European philosophy and methodology, where study groups and methodology sessions are predominantly based around the philosophy that goes beyond 'religious' thought. As a Muslim man who embodies, and deeply thinks about his faith as an everyday way of being, this is something that immediately created a drift in sense of belonging in the academia. I felt I was putting up a different face in front of my course colleagues than what I am completely as a Muslim man. In relation to specifically the postgraduate research experience I have talked more in detail about this in my chapter within this publication (see chapter 19 — Empowered Voices in Research). However, the underlying feeling of social exclusion and separation of my identity from my academic environment is something I felt resonated with other Muslim students who I spoke to as part of the focus group in drafting the Decolonise UoK manifesto.

The fact that our conversations happened in the first place in the local mosque was more telling about the level of comfort and by association discomfort that the focus group participants felt in opening up about their experiences as Muslim men in the university. This need to fall back to the mosque as a place where they feel accepted without being misunderstood or judged was important. It's a space they don't feel like they have to 'pretend' but be accepted without any preconditions; specifically, without being put in the category of 'traditional Muslim' who can easily fall under the category of a 'bad Muslim'. Instead of the 'good Muslim' who is 'liberal, moderate, and perhaps the best one — the progressive and open minded Muslim who then sometimes is also not 'really' a Muslim.[1] These categories of the 'good' , 'bad', 'moderate', 'radical' Muslim are all abstractions — constructed ideas of what those categories mean, as Yasir Moursi pens, that exist in order to mitigate 'white anxiety and fear'.[2] More than that, they are deeply colonial in nature. As Mehmood Mamdani observes, they represent descriptions of 'Muslim' other in colonial British descriptions of Muslim men of the Indian subcontinent.[3] Being Muslim somehow is never thought of as 'complex' or 'messy'[4] or heterogeneous but as a 'lumped up homogeneous identity.'[5]

This reflection isn't necessarily about what are otherwise 'explicit' forms of racism and less so about what has already been said by Wahida Ahmed and Hezhan Kader in this chapter on Muslim women's experience. What I do want to focus on is the otherwise subtle messages, presumptions, micro-aggressions, perceptions that create this constant pressure and violence on Muslim men. A violence that silences them because they feel like they can't talk about their faith through their experience of the faith — but have to constantly respond to someone else's perception of their faith. To constantly be on the defensive, and say they are not something — the constructed backward Muslim man — that they are already presumed to be. Never actually speaking of their own experiences of being Muslim and men — but always having the need to prove that they are not something everyone thinks of them being — holding them to a standard according to whiteness, of what Muslim men are and thus falling in the trap to make them feel comfortable that they are not dealing with a 'bad Muslim' but a 'good Muslim', a 'moderate'. This managing of white anxiety about 'Muslim men' is, as also in relation to the gendered construction of the 'Muslim woman', who is needs saving from the 'barbaric, uncivilized, Muslim man'.[6]

Social exclusion is subtle — but ever present — when it comes to Muslim men in the university. The reliance on the mosque as a community, while a way to feel completely comfortable, is more than often a sign that the 'outside' is not comfortable. In my discussion with Muslim men in the mosque, which was a deliberate space chosen for one of the sessions, our conversations started around our interactions outside the classroom. All the discussants agreed that their willingness to have a conversation was out of the fact that they had an implicit trust in myself and my focus group co-leader. That trust was borne out of our connection to that space — the mosque — as fellow Muslim men who knew the dangers of misunderstanding. In fact, when speaking of socialisation, the participants felt they had to take up the task of explaining to their white peers why they were dressed the way they were, why they did not drink or socialise the same way. This was because they could just sense and see the tension in their white peers' expressions, aloofness when they would manifest their 'Muslimness' in different forms.

But why do we need to constantly manage white anxiety about their perceived 'Muslimness'? Another participant in another session answered this quite simply, which was echoed in other conversations as well:

> We do not want to be misunderstood, so we would never talk in the same way to a non-Muslim. (Focus group participant)

This fear of misunderstanding is the fear of white anxiety that only looks at them through their perceived fear of the 'barbaric Muslim man'. The demonisation of Muslim students through institutional and state systems like 'Prevent',[7] and in this case, Muslim men also has this insidious effect on our psyche — it silences us. This silencing is not just a structural silencing through legislative and state measures,[8] but one which is carried on in more subtle forms I have described — in the categorisation of Muslim identity through the eyes of whiteness. It is silencing our voices, our experiences, our ability to express and our ability to think because we are constantly being asked to answer the default position. For example, 'prove you are a 'good' Muslim man'; 'Calm my, a white person's, anxieties about the fact you don't drink, you pray, you fast, you wear certain clothes'. We either calm these anxieties or we automatically become the 'radical'/'bad Muslim'. Our choice is never on our terms in these spaces of being Muslim men and are dictated by white fears and anxieties. Thus, as Muslim men, in particular, we are faced with the only choice that Moursi (citing Fanon) describes as 'Be white, or be nothing'.[9]

## Notes

1  Farah Elahi and Omar Khan (2017). *Islamophobia: Still a Challenge for Us All.* London: Runnymede Trust.

2  Yassir Morsi (2017). *Radical Skin, Moderate Masks: De-Radicalising the Muslim and Racism in Post-Racial Societies.* London: Rowman & Littlefield International.

3  Mahmood Mamdani (2002). Good Muslim, Bad Muslim: A Political

Perspective on Culture and Terrorism. *American Anthropologist* 104(3) , p. 766; Cyra Akila Choudhury (2006). Terrorists & Muslims: The Construction, Performance and Regulation of Muslim Identities in the Post-9/11 United States. *Rutgers Journal of Law and Religion* 7(3).

4  Yassir Morsi (2018). 'The 'Free Speech'of the (Un) Free'. *Continuum* 32(4), p. 474.

5  Elahi and Khan, n. 1.

6  Sunaina Maira (2009). '"Good" and "Bad" Muslim Citizens: Feminists, Terrorists, and US Orientalisms'. *Feminist Studies* 35(3), p. 631.

7  Nadine el-Nany (2019). Prevent Is Stopping Free Speech on Campus and Demonizing Muslims [online]. Available at:  https:// www.theguardian.com/commentisfree/2019/jul/01/prevent-stopping-free-speech-campus-demonising-Muslims.

8  Aislinn O'Donnell (2016). 'Securitisation, Counterterrorism and the Silencing of Dissent: The Educational Implications of Prevent' *British Journal of Educational Studies* 64(1), p. 53.

9  Morsi, n. 4 citing Frantz Fanon, *Black Skin, White Masks* (Grove press 2008).

# 13

# Two C's and a D to a First-Class Degree: Conversations with Black Men

*Anthony Otobo-Martins*
*University of British Columbia*

## Introduction

I am a regular black boy from East London. I did not go to a private school nor a grammar school. Statistically, I should be deep rooted in the black and minority ethnic (BME) attainment gap. The BME attainment gap in summary means that according to the statistics, racialised minorities underachieve significantly more than their white counterparts. Yet, I am graduating with a first-class law degree in the top ten of my year, and I have been accepted onto a Master's Degree programme in Law at the University of British Columbia in Canada. This institution only accepts twenty-five students across the globe. I am walking affirmation that relentless diligence, perseverance and determination will put you three steps closer to your ultimate ambitions and aspirations. But above all of this, the most important thing is that I am not an anomaly. There is a multitude of students who look just like me who excel academically and have remarkable career prospects. So collectively, we contribute to the university's academic standing in the league table, and yet we are undervalued, underappreciated and misrepresented.

## My Story

During secondary school, I became heavily involved in a number of sports. In spite of this, I had no intention of pursuing a career in athletics as the ultimate goal for me was still to become a Corporate Lawyer. However, during one competition, I was approached by an ex Olympian turned athletic coach who watched one of my races and saw the potential in me to make it in athletics. Soon after I began training with him rigorously, five times a week. On top of athletics, I was also heavily involved in football. From year seven until year eleven, I played for my school team as well as a local team in Chelmsford, United Kingdom. This translated to minimal revision for my GCSE examinations, but I still achieved all A*'s to B's. My GCSE results, combined with my underestimation of the difficulty of A Levels, led me to become complacent, and so I continued the subpar work ethic and increased the intensity of my athletics training. Consequently, my grades started to decline rapidly. Luckily, I have an amazing mother whom I shared my sporting dream with and she made me realise how precarious and short lived an athlete's career can be.

I remember opening my A Level results and being engulfed by this feeling of disillusionment when I saw two C's and a D. I can still feel it today. I was so disappointed, because I knew that my results were not an accurate reflection of my academic abilities. I knew that I was perfectly capable of achieving three A's, as I was. My biggest worry at that point was how my mum would react, as she has did everything in her power to ensure that I had the necessary keys to succeed in life. I was terrified to tell her that I had failed her. Fighting back tears, I walked back to my mum's car, got in and showed her my results.

My mum did not show any signs of disappointment or sadness, but consoled me and gave me several words of encouragement. I went home and checked the University and College Application System (UCAS) and saw that I had an offer from the University of Kent with the option of a place on the LLB programme.

The LLB programme at the University of Kent required a minimum grade of AAB. However, fortunately for me, the law school had the Certificate in Law programme which is a 1–year programme that is equivalent to the first year of LLB programme. Both programmes are identical in terms of modules, teaching methods and the end qualification. The distinction is that the programme is designed for students who are perceived to have potential but did not meet the entry requirements for the LLB programme. What many people do not know, is that not only did I not meet the entry requirements for the LLB programme but I did not even meet the requirements for the Certificate in Law programme. Nevertheless, Kent Law School accepted me onto the certificate course. Looking at my A Level grades on paper, your initial reaction would be that this is not a very intelligent student. But to quote Dave Chappelle:

Initial reactions are often wrong or more often incomplete, they call this phenomenon standing too close to an elephant, the analogy being that if you stand too close to an elephant, ironically you can't see the elephant.

You need to take a step back and appreciate the whole elephant in its entirety. Now in my case, on stepping back, what you would realise is that my A Level grades were not poor because I was unintelligent, rather because I just did not care enough about academics at the time as I was focusing on pursuing my sporting dreams.

The BME attainment gap is an inaccurate representation of Black, Asian and minority ethnic (BAME) students' academic abilities and confines us to a category in which we do not belong. It is a social construct with dangerous repercussions that implies a lack of intelligence. It indirectly conflates intelligence with whiteness rather than acknowledging the external factors driving the gap. My journey from my GCSE's to university effectively illustrates how misleading this equation can be.

## Speaking With Black Male Students

As part of the Decolonise University of Kent project, I held a focus group with ten young black males to discuss the attainment gap at the University of Kent. I wanted to find out why they thought it existed and what universities could do to reduce the gap. During the sessions, they stated that Induction Week is the right time to make a difference by conveying a message to students that will resonate with them.

> Induction Week is the prime time, because at that point the first-year students are filled with adrenaline and amped to begin their university experience and consequently the level of attendance is at its peak. (Focus group participant)

It is crucial that from the off, BAME students are put on the right path, with the right mentality and with the right role models to encourage a successful academic performance. The message that will be conveyed may make first-year BAME students aware of the existence of the BME attainment gap, whilst simultaneously expressing that BAME students are not incapable of success or inferior to their white counterparts. Strategies that universities can implement to achieve this are outlined in the Decolonise University of Kent manifesto. This calls for the university to give students of colour who have demonstrated academic excellence, a platform during induction week to talk about their experiences and personal successes, and to give guidance to first year students on how to attain similar achievements. Empirically speaking, I know that this is an effective method, because at the beginning of the academic year of 2018/19, I gave a talk to the first-year law students entitled 'how to survive your first year.' I also had the opportunity to speak to second-year law students and shared the strategies I used to achieve the highest grade in contract law (a course on the LLB programme).

Following both of these talks, a vast number of black students approached me to take my details, eager to replicate my success. I mentored all of them throughout the year, and these students are now all achieving 2:1s or firsts. This is a perfect illustration that BAME students are not reluctant to learn or to excel but what they need is the necessary motivation. That should begin in induction week when your audience is at its peak in order to capture the interest of as many BAME students as possible. Below are some quotes from students that were present in the lectures where I spoke:

> It was good to see someone who looked similar to me in a position where they are respected. It made me feel like I could really be successful when it comes to academics. (First-year law student)

> It is very inspiring to see someone of colour, especially as a black person to be at the optimum when it comes to grades and education. It's something you don't see very often. For me, I was star struck and realised I have an older brother who can direct me on this path called success. (Second-year law student)

> I was shocked to see another black male wearing a simple hoodie and a durag succeed in contract law, and it dawned on me that I could do it too, get the best grade wearing my hoodie and durag also. (Second-year law student)

Now if this is the impact that one lone student can have in a ten-minute talk in a lecture, then imagine the impact that ten of us would have in an hour-long lecture in induction week.

## My Perception of the BME Attainment Gap

My story becomes relevant when Dave Chappelle's principle is applied to the BME attainment gap. One's initial reaction to the gap would be that BAME students are simply academically inferior because that is what the statistics indicate. What all universities, schools, institutions and the society as a whole need to do, is take a step back and appreciate the external factors that are causing this gap (i.e. the whole elephant) and then to act. On taking a step back, one may come to realise that one factor that drives this gap is internal marking. By this I mean that the BME attainment gap persists up until a student is sixteen, and at that point the statistics are reversed and the attainment gap is flipped. This means that the grades of BAME students goes up and the grades of white students goes down. This is the case because in year eleven, exam papers nationally, are externally and anonymously marked. This is a clear indication that either consciously or unconsciously, prior to this period, teachers are marking down students of colour and thus contrary to what the BME attainment gap suggests, the problem lies with the institutions and not the individuals.

I believe another example of a driving factor for the attainment gap, as was the case for myself, may be a lack of interest in academics and/or a focus on sporting careers. Football for example, although volatile and precarious, can be an immensely lucrative career. However, we must address how we perpetuate the false pretence and feed into the fabricated narrative that black people are less intelligent and that all we are good for is excelling in sports. With this in mind though, it is vital to highlight that the fault does not lie with young black boys choosing to pursue alternative careers to academic careers. Again, the issue lies with institutional racism and the integral discrimination that permeates our society for creating the false stigma that black people are not as intelligent as white people. Without this stigma, there would be no false narrative to feed into and instead, society would simply perceive black boys entering sport as an individual pursuing a career in which he has a talent for as opposed to an individual who is pursuing a sporting career because he is not intelligent enough to become a Doctor or a Lawyer.

One irksome aspect of the perception of young black males as intellectually lesser than whites as the gap insinuates, is that it is not even a discreet or covert perception. It has become very blatant but occasionally it is decorated and disguised as celebrating black achievement. A perfect example of this is the celebration of the achievement of students from ethnic backgrounds at Brampton Manor High School in East London. *The Guardian* reported that Brampton Manor is celebrating forty-one of its students almost all from minority ethnic backgrounds who received offers to study at either the universities of Cambridge or Oxford.[1] Now part of me views this as young black excellence being acknowledged, but that part of my thought process is overridden by the part that sees this as Brampton being celebrated for achieving what was thought to be the unthinkable, i.e. getting so many young black teens into the top universities. If the former was the case, then the focal point would have been the students. They would have been the highlight of these articles, but instead the school seems to be getting most of the praise. In fact, Brampton was even labelled a 'miracle school'. This label implies that the idea of getting so many ethnic students into Oxford and Cambridge was implausible, to the extent where such a phenomenon is called a miracle. One dangerous consequence of these implications, is that it can create an inferiority complex in the minds of BAME students which acts as an almost insurmountable psychological barrier to progressing and excelling. I have personally experienced this and it takes a great deal to dismantle these barriers.

The attainment gap lies at the core of the Decolonising the Curriculum Project and was the motivating factor for me to get involved in the project. My entire race being falsely categorised as a group of people with lesser intellect irritated me because I categorically know that this is false. In order to combat this attainment gap and dismantle the psychological barriers that the BME attainment gap creates, universities, schools, and institutions need to take responsibility and take action in accordance with our manifesto.

**Notes**

1  Sally Weale (2019). London State School Says 41 Students Offered Oxbridge Place. *The Guardian* 15 January.

# 14

# Student Collectives Working for Change:
# International Reflections

*Jasmyn Sargeant*
*University of Kent*

> It is a movement on your terms, don't let others dictate the speed that which you need to create the demands of the world which should exist now. Create your own curve.
>
> (Dr Karen Salt)[1]

Coming from a background where I was easily part of the majority to being a student that was part of the minority on campus was a shift in reality. I learnt about the new culture I was immersed in and carried on with my life. There was no sense in questioning the rhythm of the curriculum, just hold your own and carry on. However, since being involved in Decolonise University of Kent (#DecoloniseUKC) project, instead of just being a student at university doing assignments, revising for exams and socialising with friends, I began to see myself having a bigger purpose than just falling into the regular university cycle. I always knew I wanted to flavour the global pot to enrich its taste for equality of opportunities, acceptance and justice but I never thought university would be the place to start.

Being drawn to the project by its name and then learning about its goal, I immediately felt like it was the right seasoning to add to the pot. It listed concerns which I had found was prevalent since starting at the University of Kent in 2016 and this was a platform for me to contribute to a cause with which I resonated deeply.

Students have great potential to be powerful agents of change. This can be exemplified through events such as the Soweto uprising where secondary school students demonstrated against the apartheid system within the education system in Soweto, South Africa (Ndlovu 2006) or the Black Power Movement in Trinidad and Tobago which started amongst undergraduate students at the University of the West Indies. The latter resisted the inequality of opportunity for Afro-Trinidadians and Indo-Trinidadians while the white populations maintained their elevated status and the government did little or nothing for dismantling such racially divided structures (Sutton 1983). Both these protests garnered national attention as the causes that they wished to highlight started among young people. This pivotal dynamism is still among the youth of today, and Decolonise University of Kent can be contemporary evidence to the power of students to effect change. This is my view having seen first-hand the effect of the project not just for change but to the student change actors.

Personally, every meeting or event we held or I attended, gave me a feeling of homeliness. I felt free to express my thoughts which allowed me to feel free to voice my most honest opinion which I would not do outside of that setting. I remember during exam deadline season being beyond stressed but looking forward to taking a break to go to a #DecoloniseUKC meeting. We were not a bunch of 'kids' up to no good but a group of activists (students and staff) who saw a problem that needed to be fixed and were energised to do the required work we thought necessary. This community feel, charged with amazing actors is the reason why the project was able to be what it is and no movement could be influential without those core components.

This has also been my experience being part of the Kent Caribbean Union where we as a student community were tired of our culture and heritage being misrepresented and overlooked. This student society was formed in 2017 to much resistance towards its conception. Despite those hiccups, in just a year and a half in operation, the society managed to invite Inspirational Speakers to speak about crucial issues such as pride in Ancestry and the Windrush generation, as well as networking events for black students on campus. This led to the society winning Group of the Year and Outstanding International/ Multicultural Initiative at the Kent Student Awards 2019. This would not have been possible without the perseverance of the founding members, particularly Louise Mayne and Jessica Mayne, who tirelessly jumped over the hurdles of getting the society started and the drive and passion for promoting positive cultural heritage from the committee members and general members of the society.

I remember being filled with pride hearing esteemed academics cite Caribbean born thinkers like C.L.R. James, Frantz Fanon, Aimé Césaire, George Padmore, Sylvia Wynter and Claudia Jones. Writers we learnt about in school being heard on a wider platform drew me to aim in getting their work presented not only at events focused on decoloniality but on core curricula where their work deserves to be.

The impact of the project was fully realised at our conference in March 2019. I remember students of various ethnic backgrounds recognising me on campus and taking the time to tell me their positive responses to the conference. Empowerment, relief and astonishment were among some of the feelings expressed. To know that other students share our same sentiments and were ready and inspired to join the movement portrays that students are ready to take on activist work alongside their intense degree courses.

**The 'International' Conversation: Perspectives of Students From the Hidden World**

While it is evident that majority of the students who study in the UK universities are UK domiciled citizens, it cannot be disputed that a decent portion of students in higher education are made up of international students not domiciled within the European Union (EU). In fact, in the academic year of 2016–2017, when I started my undergraduate degree at the University of Kent, 13% of students in higher education in the UK were International, in contrast to EU students making up 6%.[2] Considering that in most circumstances International students' tuition fees range beyond £9,250 per year, international students are very important to the neo-liberal university.

We chose to study here, so it may seem selfish to expect to learn about our own countries. However, the mission statement of the University of Kent comprises of providing education of excellent quality 'meeting the lifelong needs of a diversity of students.'[3] The mission statement of University College London, who in 2016–2017 had the largest amount of International students in the UK,[4] displays a commitment to a 'diverse intellectual community' engaged with the wider world to 'change it for the better.'[5] The mission statements tend not to vastly differ from university to university, so it can be assumed that the input of international perspectives is indispensable to higher education. Therefore, it is essential to learn about non-Eurocentric perspectives when being taught different theories, ideologies and accounts of historical experiences. It is part of the aim of the university, yet we see reading lists mainly comprising of white-British academics, with little expansion of work from Asia or Africa who form the majority of the International student population.[6] Home students could also benefit immensely from connecting with de-colonial literature whether they form part of the Asian, African or Caribbean diaspora or generally expanding their knowledge to engage with international perspectives as detailed in the University's missions statement, regardless of their ethnic origin.

Bhambra and colleagues (2018) describes decolonising as evolving thoughts to include impact of colonialism, empire and racism, to offer alternative outlooks of the world. It is difficult to effectively engage with the realistic effect of colonialism and empire without looking at literature from those countries that have faced its direct impact.

While conducting research for the #DecoloniseUKC manifesto, I led a focus group for International students of colour who currently attend the University of Kent. We all found that we had the same concerns and problem with the curriculum — the prevalence of white male theorists, who are hundreds of years old. While they may be influential to the ideologies taught, the involvement should not stop there. There should be more critiques put forward by women including women of colour, as well as literature and critique of these phenomena from an international body of writers. The students who formed part of the focus group were all from Kent Law School, a school within the university that prides itself on encouraging critical analysis. They found that decoloniality was the only aspect missing from the curriculum to encourage critical thinking.

Furthermore, the students partaking in the group felt that even in seminars their issues regarding their experience from African, Asian and Caribbean countries seemed side-lined when used for comparative purposes while issues in the United Kingdom, the European Union or the United States of America seemed more worth the discussion. This seemed to follow through assessments where students expressed that some academic staff discouraged them from including materials which they had researched about their home country or countries commonly classed as less developed. Students felt empowered and performed better in subjects where staff encouraged freedom of academic research, taught concepts outside of Western contexts and welcomed opinions based on their home experience.

Fortunately, all the international law school students in the group praised the support they were given by the administration. They found that student support was sensitive to their experiences as overseas students. Particularly, they lauded Sheree Palmer, a member of staff of colour, who is employed in the Law School, as part of its Student Success Project. Students stated that they found it easy to relate to her as she helped them seek out a proper path for their studies (which is the aim of the Student Success Project). She helped them with whatever worries or questions they had regarding their studies and future careers. This demonstrates why representation and sensitisation of issues faced by particular groups of students are important to create a sense of belonging at the university which in turn maximises their potential for success.

Bhopal, Myers and Pitkin[7] conducted research which displayed the stereotypes perpetuated by academic staff to persons of certain ethnic groups: Chinese students were thought to be quiet and passive and Black and Muslim students are considered loud, challenging and aggressive. These dangerous stereotypes perpetuate the inherent racism in the system and can hinder the success of students of colour. Staff that belong to part of the global majority ethnic groups makes all the difference for aiding in the discontinuation of these hackneyed assumptions of students of colour. This works the same for international students. Our contributions are sometimes viewed lesser based on their origin from countries in Africa, Asia, the Caribbean or Latin America. Academics that come from countries that tend to be termed as 'underdeveloped' or 'developing' provide that sort of security and representation for students to feel free to express their experiences.

Countries are intertwined. Everything that happens in one country somehow affects at least twenty others. Therefore, the critical analysis that universities expect students to demonstrate in every paper they write will be limited without different perspectives. This is why the curriculum needs to be decolonised. Inclusion of the sensitisation of international issues is actually beneficial to every single university student, regardless of their origin. This route can accurately inform students who are igno-rant of issues faced by international students OR quash the notorious myths that we have a lack of education or inappropriate infrastructure. We are just as competent and capable for success as students from the 'powerful' countries of the world. Our voices may be small but just as impactful and important.

Universities could benefit so much more from international students than just a tuition cheque. Speaking from my personal experience as a black Trinidadian woman, my primary and secondary school education has been different to the system provided in the UK. Several factors in the Caribbean Examinations Council Syllabus (the examination body which provides standardised exams for several English-speaking Caribbean countries) includes de-colonial concepts which may not be taught in other curricula. Through studying in England, I had several different culture shocks, particularly the lack of acknowledgement of Britain's colonial rule and ignorance of the exploitation of countries that were once part of the Empire. This shock is shared by a plethora of international students who come from countries that were once under a more direct colonial rule. Students coming from these countries can bring different perspectives to the curriculum through their different national lens, ones that were not blinded by the bright light of 'The White Man's Burden.'[8]

Although the consensus from the group was that administrative staff appreciated their international background, they all felt frustrated by the general student population about stereotypes attached to their countries with questions stemming from plain ignorance and/or racism and/or xenophobia. There were several events organised by the university to aid in achieving a sense of belonging for International students with the aim to bring a bond between students who move to an entirely different country and environment. However, these students most likely would not be in our seminar groups or group projects. International students are randomly allocated to a seminar group where they may meet other students who were fed the fallacy that our countries are underdeveloped which may manifest in their actions towards that student whether through micro-aggressions or blatant arrogance. The inclusion of diverse literature through readings that all students must read can aid in remodelling the preconceptions of students from countries commonly termed as 'developing' or 'underdeveloped'.

Participants in the focus group also pointed out that a perspective that fails to highlight internationally diverse literature can minoritise international students to believe that their nationality, culture and heritage are something to be ashamed of, perpetuating the rhetoric of the superiority of the (former) colonisers. Daniella Adeluwoye speaks about this same sentiment when growing up as a child in England. At home she was taught to be proud of her Nigerian heritage while in school and wider society, Africa is painted as an 'underdeveloped' continent that should be blessed to have been saved by colonisation.[9] Chimamanda Ngozi Adichie in one of her well acclaimed TED Talks speaks about how a single-story narrative through American and British books subconsciously influenced the way she wrote stories. After exposing herself to writers such as Chinua Achebe and Camara Laye, she only then realised that 'girls with skin the colour of chocolate, whose kinky hair could not form ponytails, could also exist in literature.'[10] It is disastrous that research shows that the British primary and secondary education system has failed the students of Black and Asian Minority Ethnic Backgrounds but it would be irresponsible to allow this mono-focused story to continue to be written in higher education. Our reading lists should promote positive cultural heritage by exploring and portraying the different narratives.

We talk about the colonial era and the post-colonial era but lest we forget British and French colonies still exist in the Caribbean. The rich tourists visit extraordinary five-star, non-locally owned resorts that are awashed with lusted, white, sandy beaches, clear waters and local hotel staff at their beck and call without leaving the mirage of the compound to understand the way and life of the average local citizen and how they reap little benefits from their foreign exchange. Furthermore, colonialism is still alive under the guise of Internationalisation. Treaties and constitutional rights that the UK advocates for publicly but clandestinely infringes through neo-colonialism, cannot continue to go undisturbed. A simple internet search on the Chagos Islands[11] can conceptualise this claim. In fact, I personally only learnt about the maltreatment of the citizens of the Chagos Archipelago[12] through studying public law at the University of Kent, on a module convened by Dr. Suhraiya Jivraj who is dedicated to decolonising the curriculum. We learnt about Locke and Hobbes but linking the ideologies set in British constitutionalism to the miscarriage of justice done by the UK government towards these people who were deceived into vacating their homeland. This perspective drew to the reality that all the great principles that are preached are not practised. It allowed us to critically analyse these theories which are supposed to be based in democracy, but conveniently ignored. I became attached and intrigued by this fact; it sprung my gravitation towards public law. Having debates in seminars about the issue many other students' eyes were opened and interested.

We cannot continue to teach that the World Trade Organisation (WTO) or International Monetary Fund (IMF) function to develop and improve countries without seeking profits to the detriment of several 'developing' countries who are forced to continue to be controlled by these 'Liberal' organisations. Having learnt about the major flaws in the programmes installed by the WTO and IMF in my secondary school education, this was a topic that literally hit close to home. In our first-year module, A Critical Introduction to Law, we studied Law and Economic life touching the surface on the setback of lending entities like the IMF and the World Bank. This in turn allowed me to present this matter more in depth in my independent research essay, a task in which I was hesitant to do at first but was encouraged by my seminar leader as she saw that I was passionate about the issue. Dr Hayley Gibson aided in dissipating my uncertainty about exploring the issue, which was based on fear of researching a matter in the Caribbean region. In the end I wrote my essay on how these organisations restricted the Jamaican government from appropriately facilitating the economic life of its citizens. That paper remains the highest mark that I have received throughout my university career. This proves as evidence that once a student is motivated to research issues that they are truly passionate about, their marks will reflect such. When students are exposed to topics that they can understand on a more personal level, their attainment would improve.

Decoloniality or decolonisation is not a concept/ideology that should be limited to optional modules where 'people who are concerned with those issues' have the choice to study. It can easily be integrated into a core curriculum. In contract law, I distinctly remember the head of the Kent Law School, Professor Toni Williams giving a guest lecture on Freedom of Contract where she spoke about colliding freedoms of contract, integrating case law where racism was allowed under the guise of freedom of contract as a tavern-keeper refused to serve a client because he was black.[13] I had never thought of freedom of contract as a negative concept, private individuals should be allowed to enter or refuse to enter into legally valid contracts freely, however in scenarios like described above, allowing such stimulates an undemocratic society. While the aforementioned case is Canadian and recent English jurisprudence seems to discourage such discriminatory freedom of contract, the aim of the lecture was to encourage us to critically engage with a concept that is core to contract law.

What kind of education does a University aim to provide? According to universities' mission statements, diverse intellect is formative to providing a world-class education of which UK Universities vociferously boast about. Then, we should not continue to neglect literature and thought originating from relatively newly independent countries or written by scholars from these countries.

## Notes

1  Karen Salt, Keynote Speaker, Decolonise UKC Conference (2019). https://www.youtube.com/watch?v=KYglXKq7yJ4.

2  UKCISA — International Student Advice And Guidance — International Student Statistics: UK Higher Education (2019). https://www.ukcisa.org.uk/Research--Policy/Statistics/International-student-statistics-UK-higher-education.

3  Ibid.

4  Ibid.

5  UCL Vision, Aims And Values (*About UCL* ). https://www.ucl.ac.uk/about/what/vision-aims-values.

6  UKCISA.

7  Kalwant Bhopal (2018). Social Justice, Exclusion And White Privilege In Universities. The Annual Equality Lecture with the British Sociological Association. https://vimeo.com/302226095.

8  In reference to *The White Man's Burden* by Rudyard Kipling which blatantly promotes imperialism under a guise of morality. See: Dr James Dexon (2014). *English Literature: Victorians And Moderns*. http://solr.bccampus.ca:8001/bcc/file/f373dca8-65c1-4a28-974a-035fe681f15a/1/English-Literature-Victorians-and-Moderns-1511376181.pdf#page=383.

9  Daniella Adeluwoye (2018). Who Gets To Tell Africa's Narrative? (*Varsity Online*, 2018). https://www.varsity.co.uk/features/16383.

10  Chimamanda Ngozi Adichie (2009). The Danger of a Single Story. TEDGlobal.

11  See: *R v Secretary of State for Foreign and Commonwealth Affairs, ex parte Bancoult (No 2)* [2008] UKHL 61, *Chagos Islanders v United Kingdom* (App. No. 35622/04) and *R (on the application of Bancoult (No 2) v Secretary of State for Foreign and Commonwealth Affairs* [2016] UKSC 35.

12  Granada Television, Stealing A Nation — The Plight of The Chagos Islands VS The United States (2004). https://www.youtube.com/watch?v=NVfABu61D3w.

13  *Christie v York Corporation* [1939] SCR 50.

# References

Bhambra, G., Gebrial, D. and Nişancıoğlu, N. eds. (2018). *Decolonising the University*. London: Pluto Press.

Ndlovu, S.M. (2006). *The Road to Democracy in South Africa*, Volume 2. Pretoria: UNISA Press.

Sutton, P. (1983). Black Power in Trinidad and Tobago: The 'Crisis' of 1970. 21 *The Journal of Commonwealth & Comparative Politics*.

# 15

# Intersections of Inequality: Reflections on Faith, Race and Belonging

*Hezhan Kader*
*University of Kent*

I completed my Bachelor's Degree at the University of Kent. During my first year at the university, I did not practice any religion. During my second year I started to practise Islam, and even put on the hijab (Muslim head scarf). Therefore, as someone who has been at the university as a non-practising Muslim, and as a practising Muslim, I can say that there is a difference in how inclusive the university is, depending on a student's religious beliefs.

As a non-practising Muslim, it was very easy for me to attend Freshers events and social events at the university. It didn't matter that the events were held at the university's bar, or that alcohol would be present during the social events, or that there would be a lot of free-mixing. I was able to attend anything I wanted, as it did not go against any beliefs that I held. As a practising Muslim in my second year, it became increasingly difficult for me to attend any social events. Alcohol is completely prohibited in my religion, and we are advised to even stay away from areas where alcohol will be present. Therefore, during my second and third year it was practically impossible for me to meet new people and form new friendships, as I could not attend any social events held at the university.

While staff and students are welcoming to practising Muslims, and those of other faiths, the activities and events do not show this. I believe the university focuses more on what has worked, and to them if it is not broken then it does not need fixing. However, the system is broken, and it does need fixing. It is clear that at the University of Kent, the Muslim students gain satisfaction from the inclusivity from the Islamic Society (ISOC) and the Mosque, but not from the university itself (see quotes in DecoloniseUKC manifesto from focus group on Muslim female students).

ISOC is a society that is largely aimed at engaging people who practice Islam as a religion — primarily Muslims. Therefore, alcohol and other prohibitions are not present during their social events. This means that the majority of practising Muslims are comfortable in attending such events, and being a part of the society. However, non-Muslims tend not to be part of the ISOC, so it is almost impossible to become friends with students outside of the religion, through the society. Not only this, but the Mosque that the students feel comfortable going to, is not part of the university. It is the community Mosque that so happens to be on the university campus grounds. Hence, the university cannot claim inclusivity through the Mosque, when the Mosque is separate from the university. Moreover, the Kent ISOC tends to work with the Mosque more than with the university. This is because the mosque cooperated better with the ISOC and the events they want to hold. Therefore, the university needs to understand that in order to be inclusive, they need to be more understanding of the situations and practices of the Muslim community. For example, as Muslims cannot attend events where alcohol is present, it would be much appreciated if the university held events that were alcohol-free, or during the daytime. In addition, the university needs to host events that brings religious societies and cultural societies together. Students do not get many opportunities to interact with people who are different from them, making it difficult to understand other people's stories. This means that students are stuck knowing what they have only ever known, and are not able to learn more about the world and the people in it. By hosting events that integrate different religions and cultures on campus, a space will be made to give people a better understanding of different beliefs, allowing them to form friendships they might have never expect

The university is supposed to be a place where everyone can feel accepted, and can feel comfortable enough to enter any place on campus. However, I can personally say that this is not the case for me. As someone who wears the headscarf, there is nowhere for me to go in the evenings. The only places available are the computer rooms and the library. There is no social area that I can go to after 7pm, which also allows me to follow the rules of my religion. This has resulted in feelings of isolation and exclusion from social interaction on campus, making it practically impossible to feel welcome at the university. As an 'inclusive' institution, the university needs to open spaces for people of all faiths, so that those who practise their religion can still have a place to go to, to socialise. It is important to look at all of the students who sign up to societies, and to work out how many of them actually attend their society's social events. Then, the type of students attending the event needs to be observed too. Are they predominantly white British students? Do Muslim students sign up to the societies but not attend the events? Do BAME students attend the social events? Once this is analysed, it is important to understand what happens during the events, which may not appeal to a certain group of students, and how this can be improved to make the social events more inclusive. There is no point looking at how many people from different social/cultural/religious groups sign up for societies, when it is obvious that they do not take part in the society's activities.

As someone who has studied at the University of Kent both as a non-practising Muslim and as a practising Muslim, I strongly advise the university use the current student engagement statistics in a more holistic way. This would mean looking at the engagement patterns of students from BAME, religious and cultural backgrounds and those in cultural societies in more detail. In the absence of this, the understanding of students' engagement practices may be skewed by the thoughts and feelings of the majority. As a member of the minority group on campus, I know we deserve to be heard. The university needs to start listening and it needs to start acting!

# 16

# Student–Staff Collaboration in Decolonising Reading Lists: Reflections from Change Agents

*Evangeline Ageyman and Collins Kudo-Mensah*
*University of Kent*

When Evangeline first joined the University of Kent, she had a typical student mind-set about learning. Her aims and objectives were to achieve the best grades possible, attend all lectures and seminars and organise and structure her work well. She recollects being given a seminar core reading core task, where there was an expectation to summarise the chapter and explain her understanding to fellow students. Whilst doing the reading, one never really questions particular author's views or gave it much thought as it was not the main priority. Evangeline believed she came to university to achieve the best grades possible not to diversify the curriculum. Therefore, she was not really concerned at that time as her main focus was to follow the instructions given to her by the lecturers, as she believed they were qualified and knowledgeable about the topic. In a sense, a trust was placed in their knowledge. This was naïve as Evangeline never really questioned why the curriculum was so white and whether there were any Black, Asian or minority ethnic (BAME) perspectives on these topics that were being taught. Authors such as Karl Marx, Jeremy Bentham and Emile Durkheim were all white European theorists which most social science students are encouraged to study. As a young, black student, Evangeline found this to be frustrating as this was the constant for the first two years of her degree course, where they only every slightly touched on alternative perspectives particularly from BAME backgrounds. Evangeline thought this was unfair as their voices needed to be heard within the curriculum. However, upon reflection, Evangeline began to see things differently and questioned the institution's understanding of the term diversity.

Collins and I were employed by Project Leaders Dr Barbara Adewumi and Dave S.P. Thomas to review the reading lists of undergraduate programmes taught within the School of Sociology, Social Policy and Social Research. This was conceptualised by Dave S.P. Thomas (Thomas 2020b) who works as a Project Manager on the University's Student Success Project. We were part of a new age of staff-student collaboration.

The reading list review aimed to address a gap in knowledge by firstly conducting a desk-based review of the current reading list in order to provide evidential basis for a lack of diversity in the curriculum. The audit entailed ascertaining the nationalities, gender and ethnicity of authors as well as the dates the reading lists were last updated. Categorically the most prominent of authors on the reading lists were white British and male. This prompted the familiar question, 'why is my curriculum so white? The assumption of a 'dead white male' oriented curriculum' was no longer just an assumption but proved to be the reality. By recognising and proving the disproportionate rate at which, the white British male was being represented, conversations were begun.

As part of the investigation of how students felt and engaged with their reading lists, we conducted student focus groups to explore the topic of diversity and what it meant to students. We asked undergraduate students to describe in their own words how reading lists impacted on their engagement with the curriculum? What was interesting and significant to us was being part of a project that focused on race. Students' responses highlighted the misconception of the term diversity and that everyone had a different opinion. It also raised the alarm of the limited perspectives we are presented with as students of colour. This not only signal a lack of BME authors and contributions of the global south within the reading lists, but also highlights the key issues that matter to students such as: student life, reading lists and their social environment. It was very interesting to hear students' opinions because ultimately, this was a student-led project which was designed for the students by the students. Making sure their voices were heard was essential to the project.

Within the focus groups there was a consensus that students were not aware that contributing or changing the reading list was an option; this was reminiscent of my younger self as a student. There was also an assumption that the reading list was white British male-oriented, and their truth or research was absolute. So, is the knowledge we are presented with in university authentic? Well, based on the reading lists we would say it is skewed, but the lenses can be adjusted through projects such as this one and hearing students' voices on the matter, particularly BAME students. If we have learnt anything, we have learnt that knowledge holds power which is meant to be liberating not stagnant or restricted. Focus groups highlighted the cruciality of the students' voices not only to improve engagement, but also informing students that the university genuinely care about their thoughts and opinions on the matter. Hearing their counter-narratives and lived experiences made us realise that change was a necessity.

Having reviewed the reading lists, we developed research skills that pushed and challenged us to think far more deeply about what and how knowledge is taught. Collins subsequently went on to do a dissertation that sought to understand the extet to which drill music was the cause of recent rise of violence in the UK (or not). Collins recalls how he developed a new and practical knowledge of critical race theory (CRT) which provided a framework to construct key critical debates and obtain a balanced perception of authors (both white and BME) within his thesis. An ability to challenge power with new knowledge of CRT was key to understanding the need to decolonise the curriculum through liberating students' knowledge and presenting a more diverse reading list. What constitutes 'authentic knowledge' should not be placed solely in the hands of neo-liberalised higher education institutions who are in a privileged position to decide for all.

At the Medway campus the explanation of the project was more orientated to academics, which was significant in generating awareness. Engaging with the creators of the reading lists was integral in eliciting the much-needed change and natural progression. Speaking at conferences and events was also a crucial part of the process. Visiting the Canterbury campus gave us a bigger platform to speak to students; this was encouraging. We used this opportunity to reinforce the importance of students seeing themselves represented in the curriculum. This was ironic, considering the greater proportion of BAME students studied at the Medway campus. The difficulty in the student engagement in the Medway campus was highlighted when recruiting students for the focus groups. We found the most effective way was to speak directly to students was at the end of their seminar or lecture classes. The transition from the Medway to Canterbury campus was inspiring, as students like me, students of BAME backgrounds, genders and sexuality, were promoting such a project and making active strides pressing for change. Students were unapologetically demanding change.

There are many components to decolonising the curriculum, which the reading list review project made us realise. This project is bigger than us. It was a movement which needs to be continued and developed. With this role we knew we were in a privileged position. We had empirical evidence proving the racial and gender-based composition of our reading lists. This information ought to be publicised to reiterate the need for diversity within the curriculum

## References

Thomas, D. (2020). Democracy, Diversity and Decolonisation: Staff-Student Partnerships in a Reading List Review [Online]. Available at: https://www.advance-he.ac.uk/news-and-views/Democracy-Diversity-and-Decolonisation.

# 17

# The Audacity to Occupy Spaces and Contribute to Knowledge

*Lisa Shoko*
*University of Kent*

The Decolonise the Curriculum project at the University of Kent gave students an opportunity to openly explore and investigate the ways in which the university could begin tackling issues raised by students of colour on campus including experiences of racism in the classroom. Some students had the feeling of obligation and burden when asked by lecturers and other students to comment on issues of race as if they were an authority on the issue, and only through these discussions did some students realise that their experiences with campus security were significantly different to those of their white counterparts. Where white students were met with understanding and tolerance, students of colour were usually met with impatience, intolerance and sometimes violence.

Students from the project used the platform to criticise some of the issues presented by the Equality Challenge Unit in their 'Equality in Higher Education' report (2017). They were specifically concerned with the claim that students from Black, Asian and minority ethnic (BAME) backgrounds were underperforming in comparison to their white counterparts, without any clear reasoning to justify this. In response to this report, we as students conducted twelve focus groups. Through Decolonise the University of Kent we engaged with our peers, the majority of whom were from BAME backgrounds, to learn what they understood about the intersections between race and higher education and what they thought about the Equality in Higher Education report (2017). We wanted to know what arose for them from the idea of a BAME 'attainment gap' and whether it was to the benefit or detriment of students of colour. The findings from our focus groups and interviews informed our manifesto, which we presented to Kent and other universities as part of a broader movement of student activism in support of decolonising Higher Education institutions. What we challenged was the idea of an attainment gap, what it meant, why it existed and what was responsible for this disparity in final degree outcomes between students of colour and their white counterparts.

It was surprising for some students that although they had a decorated education history, here at University they were considered to be unambitious, unintelligent, and a statistic fallen through the attainment gap. However, other students were comfortable talking about their experiences of Blackness and racialisation on campus, as if the claims in the report were only to be expected. These students thought that this was evidence of persistent institutional racism, and challenged the recurring themes that they had seen historically marginalised people experience (e.g. colonisation, Windrush, the slave trade) and the traumas that they lived through as the descendants of those people. Whilst the statistics provided by the 2017 report suggested that students from BAME backgrounds were underperforming, there was very little, if any consideration of the role that Higher Education institutions played in impacting BAME students' experiences of erasure on campus. There was also no consideration for the significance of a lack of culturally appropriate mental health and well-being support for students from these backgrounds. The report did not account for why students who entered the academy with exceptional grades and were predicted to finish with a First class or 2:1 degree did not. The information provided, suggested that they were not putting in enough effort.

I found myself often reflecting on how I was raised and how, despite rigorous instruction and zeal, I had fallen through the 'gap'. I thought carefully about the path that had led me here. I thought especially about my grandparents who raised me and the effort that they put into my upbringing. Both of them being educators, had always found creative ways of inspiring learning, especially since I was head-over-heels for tennis and was not seasoned at balancing the different aspects of my life. Despite my being distracted, both grandparents encouraged me to pursue my studies and look beyond my athletic ability and were often forced to be creative in helping facilitate this. Literature was the love that my grandfather lent me. He always brought back books that were above my reading level and challenged me to elevate. The best of these was Takadini (1997). It is an inspired narrative about marginalised communities within the context of my tribe (Shona). This book deals with the challenges of being a woman in the Shona culture and the fear and taboo surrounding albinism. I am privileged to have engaged with and to have been brought to such a book by my grandfather. Ironically, I find myself living on the fringes and trying to earn my position as the main characters in that book did. Even with all this privilege, I find myself constrained by a system that is solely focussed on my Blackness.

Students' views in the focus groups refuted the opinion of the Equality in Higher Education Report (2017) — that the disparity was an issue of race or rather the ethnicity of the individual students. Rather, the consensus was that these claims were unfounded and alarming because they had similar undertones to colonisation and perpetuated racialised ideas of the inferiority of non-white people. Students gave various examples of where this rang true for them including from literature they had to read on courses or at school. Like Rudyard Kipling's 'The White Man's Burden' (1899). The BAME attainment gap rhetoric felt like a re-hash of European imperialism propaganda enlisting the West to save the uneducated and underdeveloped Africans articulated in the likes of Kipling's seminal work. The myth that Africans were uncultured, uncivilised and needed to be introduced to Western thought in order to be recognised (more than savages) undoubtedly fuelled white supremacist thought. In order to fit in, the 'savages' of the dark continent would have to abandon their heritage, customs, traditions, dress and adopt Western ones in order to be embraced by their oppressors as adequate. We as students in the focus groups felt the analogies all too vividly. After all it was our families that were affected by Windrush, Prevent and other aspects of the hostile environment.

The attainment gap flagged BAME students yet again as needing help, needing to be 'saved' from low intellectual and vocational achievement. Whilst we understand that everyone needs help sometimes, the Equality in Higher Education Report (2017) seemingly implied that the 'deficit' of each student's achievement came down to the shades of their skin. This did not ring true to our experiences as students of colour in the UK. The premise of the attainment gap thesis invalidates identities and does not take into consideration that the University constantly fails students of colour by not providing them with safe spaces where they can embrace their ethnicity as part of their identity without prejudice and feel as if they belong, without prejudice. On the contrary, our experiences were that our white peers hardly encounter spaces where they feel discriminated against in the same ways, especially on campus. Moreover, even if things did happen, they had more choices and liberty to leave that space, without looking too hard and delve into the comfort of every other space that exists to validate their identity and their experiences — a luxury that BAME students are so often denied.

One example is in relation to sports at university where many of us came with the hope of continuing and going further in our chosen sports from school. However, we can often struggle to play the sport which we had excelled in and/or loved because of explicitly feeling that we did not belong in that space, with that team. Rather we were treated as outsiders, perceived as being too aggressive, perhaps you know, like Serena Williams in tennis. As BAME students, we could be seen as too competitive, too loud after celebrating a great volley shot over the net. There were no other visible women of colour playing on teams, no coaches either. We, along with others in similar situations, stopped enjoying the sports we had wanted to play. The feeling of being visible and yet invisible at the same time, always noticed but often overlooked is difficult to know how to tackle. We often struggle to find where we belong. This can lead to feeling like you cannot 'hack' the demands of university life. Validation or achievements from the past can become a false narrative which ends up feeling like one is being set up for failure when you get to University and can no longer prove yourself amongst huge cohorts of other students. Often many students may feel that they have been lulled into a false sense of security, if they have achieved at school but then not necessarily good enough to thrive at University.

As a result of the Decolonising the Curriculum project, we had opportunities to come together for the focus group cafes as well as for other meetings and events, including reading groups and, in particular, a masterclass with Professor Gurminder Bhambra, the first Decolonial Studies professor in the UK. Through these moments we started dismantling what we already felt to be untruths, like the attainment gap narrative. We began to understand and explore issues from marking biases at university level, which are more often absent in secondary school because of external anonymous marking, to thinking about the evidence on how important a sense of belonging is for all students to perform well. This would include the need to tackle and provide spaces and opportunities in music, sports, societies and elsewhere to which  students of colour felt they belonged and would not be treated like an outsider. However, we did all agree that relying on societies and extra-curricular activities to meet the equitable demands of BAME students without making any institutional changes would impede the overall goal — some belonging does not amount to a sustainable model for legitimate belonging.

The Decolonise the Curriculum Project facilitated by Dr. Suhraiya Jivraj was a transformative space that manifested through group chats, conversations in the Centre for Sexuality, Race and Gender Justice (SeRGJ), collaborations, podcasts and zines. There are many other ways in which this project inspired innovation, creativity, confidence and most importantly friendship and a sense of community. The project was a place where I was not burdened by my Blackness but instead, where I found my solace, validation, appreciation and the feeling that my experiences were worthy of belief. More than that, they were worthy of being recorded as truth. Even when you are the only person in the room sitting in silence, the Centre for Sexuality, Race and Gender Justice made me feel embraced, included and represented. There was strength in the colour of our skin which we had come to understand did not warrant exclusion. Dr. Jivraj successfully created a breeding ground for excellence by allowing us to be the deepest-rooted versions of ourselves and making us feel like we belonged.[1]

There are subtle nuances that cannot be captured in words about the inelegance of race and the experience of being a racialised person, and as such, it is difficult to encapsulate the true feeling of what it means to be part of a project such as this. There was a time not long before the project started, where my confidence was so low that even with a background of public speaking and debating, I couldn't articulate myself. I would always hesitate when spoken to and be overwhelmed by anxiety of doing so that I would start flailing for responses and begin stuttering and stammering, all of which did not start until I started attending university. However, by the end of the first year of the project, I had performed exceptionally well as a researcher, focus group leader, conference organiser and speaker. I have been able to translate my owned lived experiences into research and publications and use that as a tool to speak truth to power and advocate for more equitable conditions for students of colour to achieve.

Some of what we used to do to get the most of our learning experiences was to go on excursions together. One of these trips involved visiting the Building the Anti-racist Classroom Collective at Queen Mary's University of London.[2] When we arrived there, there was a sense of familiarity in the atmosphere. We were sitting in a yurt on the floor with colourful cushions to make it more comfortable. The place we were in had the right energy that I can only compare to other places that we had been together especially in the Centre for Sexuality, Equality, Race and Gender Justice. More than being invited into the room, I felt that there was a willingness from us to learn and a willingness from the Building the Anti-racist Classroom Collective to listen, which made it a learning experience for all those who were involved. It was like a ritual that we performed turning our traumas and experiences into transformative tools which can be leveraged to inspire other people to engage with race more conscientiously. These were people who were trying to further 'the conversation' about race in an educational way that refused to silence the voices of people of colour like me; and they were not only willing to impart knowledge, but also to listen to whatever contributions any of us wanted to make. It was like being teased — we were being dared to have the audacity to create a design for what equity at the University might look like; we were being dared to have the audacity to occupy spaces on campus and to contribute to knowledge.

One of the findings that emerged from our focus groups was that there was a significant gap that needed to be filled when it came to students of colour achieving a sense of belonging on the university campus. With that in mind Ahmed Memon and I were inspired to plan and bring to life something that reflected the environment that we had benefitted from in the Centre for Sexuality, Equality, Race and Gender Justice and again as guests on the Queen Mary University of London campus. We wanted to establish a principled space predominantly created for students of colour in which they would have control of activities and the feelings created within it. We also wanted students who participated to equally benefit from the protection that we found within the spaces in which we were inspired to explore the curiosities of our experiences and vulnerably reflect on those experiences in a way that would wholesomely reflect on what we could offer to the Kaleidoscope Hub. The design was planned around creating healthier help-seeking behaviours amongst students of colour, by providing them with a specific zine that instructed them on where to go to on campus to locate e.g. then Kent Union BAME Network, the new Kaleidoscope Network, the student well-being centre etc.

Working with the project I have been challenged to be brave and daring even in the face of strong adversity. This is something that I hope to continue doing beyond my undergraduate degree. The details of how our stories and Manifesto will be used to further the decolonising movement at the University of Kent is yet to be seen.

Who will speak for those who are not yet ready to speak for themselves if I do not have the audacity to occupy spaces? Who will inspire them to do so, if I do not write vulnerably about my own experiences, and the shedding of mistruths that led to my empowerment?

## Notes

1 A high majority of the students from Decolonise the Curriculum graduated with a First Class or a 2:1 degree and were recognised through multiple awards at the graduation ceremony for their performance and contributions to the University.

2 When we were hosted by Building the Anti-Racist Classroom (BARC) Collective.

# 18

# Empowered Voices in Research: The Road to the Forum on Ethics of Research

*Ahmed Raza Memon*
*University of Kent*

Power to those that sweep the streets, with more knowledge than PhDs

(Lowkey, 'Letter to the 1%')

## Research: For the Greater Good? The Paradox

The PhD process as a program for an academic in training, or research in academia, is burdened by the question; what good is it and what is the 'impact' of this research. The idea of a greater good is a consistent and constant indictor of the 'value' of the research a PhD student or academic undertakes. Concerns that it should speak to a 'broader audience', to policy makers, lawyers and even more importantly to 'those with whom one is in conversation with' i.e. established academics in the field. Even if greater good or the purpose of academic training is recognised through the engagement of scholarship beyond its bubble, the concept of research itself or what the researcher does are not questioned on a fundamental level. It is possible, for example, to explain how something has 'value' and yet another to question who decides this 'value'? Do the communities, people and groups for whom the 'value' is determined want to be researched at all?

PhDs and in fact academic journal articles are written by and for academics. Academia is a career and like any career; it is embedded in ideas of stepping up a career ladder. Showing 'value'. 'impact', and 'public engagement' are just as much of a tick-box system and the crux of academic training at the graduate level.

## Decolonising Research Collective: A Breathing Space — the Beginning?

The decolonising research collective of the postgraduate research students started from a specific set of questions that arose from a conversation with a colleague in the University of Kent Law school around the research methodology in the PhD program. The idea of a collective was to establish a space for research students to share our experiences and reflection on our respective projects. Specifically, thinking about how we have struggled to frame our project in a way which is anchored in relation to decolonisation itself. This included focused readings on scholars from non-European and non-white knowledge which would take the form of poetry, literature, video clips or material collated by activist groups based in the global south. We recognised that the space was meant to have conversations that were both substantive in nature i.e. what sources we use to present knowledge from the global south as well as have more material, institutional change in PhD training and research environment (Naqvi et al. 2019).

Our approach was not to only frame this as a 'reading group' where we just discuss readings. Dr. Priya Hope made clear certain ground rules about what decolonisation meant in form of the space in which we have the conversations as well. The first meeting led to the drafting of an ethos document outlining the aims and guiding principles of the space. Without quite intending to, we ended up creating a space which was not removed from our personal/political racialised experiences. This recognition of course is an inherent one among people who have gendered/racialised experience within the academic community. It is precisely why research students and staff of colour remain marginalised to the 'white male' academic standard as the only standard of excellence. As Jason Arday (2017) writes in his report for the University and College Union on 'Exploring black and minority ethnic doctoral students' perceptions of an academic career', most doctoral students indicated that they felt that 'equal access to the academy did not exist for individual from ethnic minority background'. If our collective's space were to be explicitly 'decolonial', it automatically needed to protect and buffer us against the same micro-aggressions, appropriations, misrepresentations and emotional labour that we face within the academia. Being conscious of how the space we occupy, the people in those spaces, can easily push us to the margins of the conversations by de-centering our voices, we created guiding principles of the Decolonise Research Collective.

There were four main principles we wanted to abide by from the outset. First, that representation was key, which meant that voices mattered. Most importantly, we wanted to make that voices of researcher students of colour was centred in the room, given that the space was not openly exclusive to just PhD.

The second principle was to decolonise the way we write and communicate our ideas. We wanted to develop our own way of writing beyond expert vocabulary and jargon in the process of 'writing' and 'feedback' sessions. This was in spirit of the broader idea that we were within a system which was far removed from the material spaces where knowledge is experienced. So we needed to recognise that language becomes a marker of 'expertise' to demarcate between the academic who knows and the 'subject of research who does not. Even as researcher students of colour, who felt that our own professional space marginalised us, our recognition to accept our 'academic privileged' position was a conscious way to accept our own responsibility as researchers. To specifically not reiterate ideas of 'expertise' we thought were rooted in colonialist 'research'.

Linked to language and decolonising writing, but also in communicating our ideas, we aimed to keep the verbal, written engagement as accessible as we could out of respect to the ethic of decolonisation. This ethic, in terms of communication, relates to the position we occupy as 'academics' in this university located in the North, talking about base realities that we do not (might not have ever) experienced. It was our effort to develop our way of writing/communication so that at some level we communicate with the practice of speak 'with' and not speak 'to' the subjects/concerns of our studies.

Our final principle was respecting the space, as a collective on decolonising research our intention is to respect the aims of the space which means being aware of and actively engaging with reading, writing, researching from a positionality of the south. There needs to be active distancing from representations, methods, knowledge structures that are Eurocentric in nature or form. Thus, our selections for the collective's sessions were by scholars from the global south, knowledge that was not 'scholarly' or 'academic' in nature but spoke about stories of violence by oppressive systems as well those that resisted those stories. We wanted to also explore poetry, literature, documentaries on indigenous resistance, activist literature against oppressive systems.

**Is Research Colonial? the Journey to the Ethics Forum**

The decolonising research collective was more than just a reading group for us — we wanted to think more deeply, within the confines of our precarious position as PhDs and hourly-paid lecturers, about our praxis within that space. Our plan was to set up a workshop on having a conversation around our experiences of doing research and our challenges in doing it in a way where it ultimately raises broader problems of its 'colonial' nature and 'power' in creating knowledge about material realities of communities and people within the academic university.

As we were organising for this, it was quite clear to me that planning an informal discussion session as a PhD. Student with no publication, and therefore no particular academic profile was itself a hindrance. I put down a list of academics I believed could be good for a panel. Unfortunately, of the five academics I had contacted, except for two replies who could not commit to the day, the rest did not even reply. I ended up relying on Dr. Suhraiya Jivraj and Professor Toni Williams in giving suggestions and specifically referring to them in my email to the academics that did eventually become part of the session — which ended up being an 'informal discussion forum'.

The shift from a panel to an informal discussion forum came out of a conversation with Dr. Karen Salt. She reiterated that we need to start thinking about the space beyond just a place where experts talk about something. Rather, she suggested a sharing of experiences from which we can reflect and learn and carry forward into something 'actionable', even if at the most individual level for people attending the session. This particular idea is what led to the informal discussion forum being a place where five researchers shared their experiences and reflections of what 'ethics' of research meant for them.

**Decolonising Knowledge — Reflections on the Journey**

In the course of the discussion forum, the one thing that stood out most was the importance of lived knowledge. The idea of lived knowledge and its absence in academia is what spoke to me in understanding that research is colonial in nature. The colonial university utilises research to 'label', 'intellectualise' and treat the 'human' as the 'subject' to be studied (Smith 2013). This framing, as Linda Tuhiwai Smith (Ibid.) points out in her brilliant book *Decolonizing Methodologies*, is colonial at its heart and can be seen how historically research is deployed in this particular way by colonial anthropologists, geographers, thinkers to justify the colonial enterprise itself. Therefore, research in the university is colonial in nature because knowledge, or what we consider and recognise as legitimate knowledge, is colonial in nature. Decolonising research — as an endeavour itself is not just about reading authors from the global south (even though that centring of 'othered' voices is important part of it), it needs to be inextricably linked to how we experience our 'academic spaces'. Knowledge cannot be compartmentalised into legitimate and a somehow lesser form of knowledge. Decolonising research needs to tackle the challenge of decolonising knowledge. This means continuing to reflect not just our own lived experiences within the academia, but also those outside of it, beyond the reading list. Ultimately presenting the provocation of what is considered a 'legitimate' source of knowledge and who produces this knowledge to claim 'expertise'.

This provocation would strike at the heart of deconstructing the identity that we all as researchers maintain and create, of a 'researcher/ academic'. Thus, at its most fundamental level we must deconstruct what it means to be an 'academic/researcher' — and therefore re-purpose our approach to creating a space for anti-colonial resistance against the colonial university. In the sections that follow on, I consider what is required in carving out a space for this resistance and how through this resistance we can redefine and re-construct the 'colonial self-entitled researcher'. What is required is thinking about how this 'self-entitled researcher' is constructed in a specific academic ecosystem. Thus, understanding the construction of the 'self-entitled colonial researcher' through a sociologically grounded way helps us in thinking about resistance through these modes of sociological ecosystem of the academia.

**Re-Existing Through Practice: Writing 'With' Not 'About'**

Decolonising research cannot be just an intellectual endeavour. The very idea of only decolonising within the frames of intellectual 'discussion' is a failure of imagination. In the practice of decolonisation there must be the synergy of action and thought in understanding that knowledge is both thought and praxis not simply a separation of the 'mind' from the 'body'. The 'mind' here is with reference to the knowing researcher and the 'body' as the object of study i.e. the communities. This binarisation of 'thought' of the knowing researcher out to 'study' and explain the 'object' is at the heart of colonialism. Within the research environment of the University, there is an implicit framing of 'subject' of the research and the 'observer' researcher as the 'outsider' (Smith 2013). At a fundamental level it represents a certain relation that is the basis of how the idea of researching is defined and justified — as a scientific exercise of the observer as an objective individual collecting 'data' on the subject, analysing it to produce knowledge *about/on* the 'subject' of the research. This binarisation continues to be reflected in the way we do and understand research at the University. Decolonising knowledge itself requires a questioning of the main premise of University education as being colonial in nature. It has to then also engage with and take form of a new re-existence within the colonial university. This re-existence is, as Dr. Karen Salt reminded us[1] — and as Remi Joseph-Salisbury (2018) observes, in how we speak 'truth' to power. Speaking 'truth to power' here refers not just in grand gestures, but more importantly also in everyday praxis.

Perhaps in order to understand this practice of decolonising knowledge we can turn to Franz Fanon (2008) and Allama Iqbal (Sevea 2012). Fanon and Iqbal called on 'native elites' to listen, value, reflect and learn from their own communities who they must work with and not speak for or separate from in their endeavour against colonialism. In the context of British colonial rule Iqbal spoke of a consciousness of Muslim mind and spirit which grew *with* the struggles of the 'common' man, the peasant, beyond caste/tribe differences. His critique of Muslim public intellectuals at the time was that they grew apart from the struggles of those less privileged in order to respond the construction of the 'Muslim' man created by the white gaze of British colonialism at the time (Iqbal 1940). This construction of Muslim man as the savage, illiterate became a internalised struggle where the Muslim intellectual became fixated to prove they are not 'savage'. For Iqbal, this only reiterated the gaze of the 'west' and his entire epistemological basis for a Muslim consciousness was a re-existence of Muslim 'self' or 'khudi' (in urdu; Ibid.) on its own terms as a struggle against colonialism. This struggle required the Muslim intellectual to work with, learn from and apply their mind to the everyday struggle against imperialism that labourers, workers, those less privileged were constantly engaged in colonial India. The internalised gaze of whiteness in the black man is what Fanon (2008) then referred to when he spoke of the 'native intellectual'. The native intellectual internalised 'whiteness' to such an extent as to loath their own community, trying only to speak to the inferiority that whiteness has constructed of their world. For Fanon just like Iqbal, the struggle for decolonisation was also a re-existence or consciousness beyond the 'white gaze'.

We could understand the academy both as a microcosm of a colonial structure and part of the way in which power operates to perpetuate racism, sexism and knowledge hierarchies similar to colonial structures. If I had not known a mentor who was willing to navigate those corridors of power through their own networks of scholar activists, I would not have been able to pull the workshop together — or be introduced to be people who were thinking along similar lines. The invisible college works both ways but the neoliberal academy only values those that perpetuate its colonial structure — and it is the PhDs, early career researchers who are caught within this systemic 'isolation' and/or 'alienation'. Unless they are either pressured to 'assimilate' to, as Fanon put it 'be white or be nothing' (Ibid.). The nothingness here is the condition and danger of precarity for PhD's that is exacerbated by isolationism. The operational mode of 'being white' is to be subsumed as the 'neo-liberal' academic who thrives and succeeds in the academic networks of 'intellectual elites'.

These lessons ring true still when I reflect on Dr. Salt's brilliant keynote in the Decolonise UoK conference, March 2019.[2] Dr. Salt spoke of our need to think about what does it mean to live in a truly ethical, decolonial way as 'academics'. How do we treat the sweeper in our corridor, how is it we treat our juniors. How do mentors, seniors support their precarious and early career staff without expecting some kind of 'career' return. Does our 'theory' reflect in our everyday 'praxis' or rather — should we even have the binary between theory and praxis. Instead we should think about the scholar activist as a person who, like Fanon and Iqbals' vision of the intellectual, constantly reflects, learn with and from the community around them. Hence, these everyday encounters of us 'existing' in the academia are all interwoven into the way we talk about 'decoloniality'. Since if we are truly to create a space within what is otherwise historically a colonial endeavour and now increasingly part of a 'neo-liberal' system, we need to start acting in a way that reflects the 'intellectual' conversations that speak to those values. Otherwise, those 'values' spoken in an intellectual way simply become conversations being had outside the experience of our material realities. Perhaps, that is the modus operandi of the colonial university; to have 'elites' who call themselves experts of knowledge themselves perpetuate hierarchies, elitism, faux objectivity in the name of 'research'. 'Research' that is devoid of 'body', 'experience', 'practice' and everyday resistance.

To decolonise research through practising it is an active mode of resistance — remembering you are not alone and to create, thrive, re-exist in networks of resistance. PhD students and early career researchers are where that space is most effective as you can mould, shape, and subsume the student, precarious researcher into whatever form 'white' academia wants it to take to maintain its status quo. At the same time, it is also the same place where the scholar activist could be supported to become an intellectual who embodies anti-racist, anti-sexist and decolonial praxis in not just re-forming themselves as a 'scholar activist' but also as a teacher. In order to resist that 'colonisation' of the PhD students mind, what is then important is support networks of scholar activists who embody, understand and are actively creating work that is conscious of decolonisation work as more than just intellectual academic exercise. The role of mentors and senior academics who are scholar activists is crucial to the success and support of decolonising research spaces and efforts.

## Reframing the Vocabulary of the 'Conversation' — Beyond the White 'Gaze'

Another equally important reflection in relation to decolonising knowledge as both practice and theory is pushing the decolonisation vocabulary beyond whiteness. Reframing the vocabulary has psychological, intellectual and emotional effects on 'BAME' PhD students. Taking my own positionality as an example, I want to demonstrate in this section about my reflections how 'theory' is deeply intertwined with everyday experience. More importantly, how the false binary between the two effects BAME PhD students even more so as they are asked to intellectualise what is essentially their everyday material experience. In my case, my faith, both in practice and as a way of thinking through intellectual thought, is something I never saw being put forward as actual philosophy. If my project isn't specifically on something to do with 'Islamic legal thought', I didn't find the space where Islamic thought, practice, experience could ever be a way of thinking through other issues surrounding us. We could think about social inequality, critical thinking, or even international law through European frames and philosophies — but somehow thinking about anything outside, it becomes a 'speciality' of its own, something restricted to a place, person (Morsi 2018). We are asked to become academics and engaged with 'critical thought' but that critical thought as a way of viewing the world and law is limited to Europe's 'white' gaze on the world (Dabashi 2015).

The white gaze is apparently the only gaze through which we can understand the whole world — but no other gaze can be used to learn something about the rest of the world. That is perhaps why I could never have conversations about my faith, my everyday practice without having the fear of either being judged for 'believing' and also being a 'critical researcher'. That is exactly why the 'mosque' became a space where I could live this 'other world', the part of me that wants to feel accepted for my faith as well.

Being a Muslim PhD student felt often like a place of living in-between two worlds even though my experience was embodied, everyday — not something that could be split neatly into these two different 'epistemes' or ways of living my reality. Members of our collective, through conversations with the Law School's postgraduate research staff team, managed to get some decolonial philosophy (Mignolo 2009) as part of study group reading. This still perhaps is not enough as it comes from the limited, yet important, aspect that we need more diverse/decolonised opinions. However, they are still referred to as about something called 'decolonisation' simply as a 'metaphor' (Tuck et al. 2012 ) or a 'good' thing to do without the appreciation that this 'theory' is often how we reflect on our everyday experiences and the spaces we occupy. More importantly perhaps, that we can learn so much through the reflection of our everyday experiences as people of colour about these decolonial theories by brilliant scholars of colour.

To simply talk of decolonisation in theoretical or intellectual ways as if it is only an ethereal philosophy anyone can tap into while reflecting about their work is to remove the ethical question we are confronted with when talking of decolonisation. This ethical question is not one which rests on 'who' can do decolonial theory, but rather 'how' can one do decolonial theory ethically. The burden of the 'how' lies on those whose relation to knowledge centred at the university and in society i.e. the white academic or even those that have an imperial relation to the marginalised within their communities i.e. upper caste brown academics. This question of the 'how' is even more important than the why we must do it because of the material, structural and political reality of colonialisation and its neo-imperial forms existing in the world today and more importantly, in the form of the colonial university. These realities are more often than not a product of years, generations of colonial trauma, survival, re-existence and finding our voice through the orientalising, colonising, fetishising gaze of European white scholarship. When we talk about decolonising research, we must talk about who gets to speak about it in 'what' way, how must those that benefit from the structure or are historically centred talk about it, and who embodies it and has lived through these realities in different ways.

This question is for me a question of ethics of 'research' itself. It is a conversational, dialogical mediation between positionalities of power. For a decolonial research, we need to engage in this mediation, which then needs to be set through principles. Our broader project around Kaleidoscope Network and hub includes such principles[3] we must engage in, in order to even practise decoloniality. The same should and in fact in different form has been said of research and knowledge production. Beyond whiteness as an overarching imperial form, the idea of ethics in research has also been explored on the topic of 'caste'. Caste as a form of colonial relation in the Indian subcontinent has existed in the subcontinent long before British Colonisation where socio-economic hierarchy of 'human' (i.e. an upper caste Brahmin) less human (lower caste), and non-human (untouchable or Dalit) is based on spirituality and blood lineage (Ambedkar 1948). It is not only present within Hindu faith, but also reproduced in other faith practices within the subcontinent including Islamic, Christian, Sikh context (see, for example, Ahmad 1978 and Puri 2003). Conversation around research of caste as an over-arching reality of brown communities both in India, Pakistan and the west have ended up producing conversations around the ethics of speaking about these experiences i.e. who gets to speak about these experiences and how. Most notably in the context of caste research through a co-authored dialogic book 'The Cracked Mirror' by Dalit academic Gopal Guru and non-Dalit Professor Sundar Surrakai (2018). Surrakai and Guru speak of the ethics of writing about caste oppression and experience especially when Brahmin/upper caste researchers write as not only outsiders but as those historically, structurally and politically privileged. For Guru and Surrakai, in order to understand the 'whole' experience, both the power holders ( i.e. the non Dalit Brahmin) deconstruction of his/her power and the Dalit experience are important. Both aspects can give a full knowledge in dialogue with each other. However, at the centre of this dialogue for Guru and Surrakai, regardless of their positionalities, the ethical goal of research on caste has to be the dismantling of caste supremacy as imagined by Dalit leader and scholar B.R. Ambedkar (2014). The research thus has to be led by, framed in its objective by those colonised. In a similar vein, whiteness in a way in which it can be deconstructed needs the active participation of the white scholar. However, the overarching goals need to be set as dismantling 'whiteness' and the 'white gaze' — not to reinforce, or invisibilise it. It is particularly this goal of deconstructing and dismantling the dominant/colonising frame as the objective of decolonisation. Dia da Costa and Alexandere Da Costa (2019) and Shaista Patel (2016) attempt to answer this question of 'how' one does decolonial research through a conceptual framing of 'multiple colonialisms' in society i.e. whiteness, Brahminism (casteism), anti-blackness and anti-indigeneity. For Da Costa and Da Costa (2019) and Patel (2016), we must find ways in which to create decolonial solidarities beyond identities but with the ethical imperative of dismantling any/all colonial power frames. This then requires those of us who occupy those positions in relation to 'colonised' to deconstruct our positionalities critically to that end i.e. white scholars deconstructing whiteness, non-black scholars of colour deconstructing anti-blackness and upper caste scholars of colour critically reflecting/critiquing caste supremacy.

This discussion on ethics is also central to the claim that Fanon and Iqbal make in their critique of the native elite who is effectively the person of colour internalising and operating within the logics of 'whiteness'. Simply stating that only scholars of colour 'can' do decolonial scholarship is to sweep Fanon and Iqbal's critique of internalised 'whiteness' under the rug. It easily turn to 'performativity' as measure of progress as Sara Ahmed (2004) points out. This 'performativity' is exactly what the neo-liberal university, and 'native elites' utilise to their own ends. Thus in re-making the academic researcher as a anti-colonial researcher, one must be wary of internalisations of whiteness as well as invibilisation of any/other forms of colonial frames the researchers actively avoid. This is especially in the case of researchers of colour, as Dalit and non-Dalit scholars/activists in India point out, who do not talk about caste structure as a colonial frame (Krishnaswamy 2005; Jangam 2015; Figueira 2008). This invisiblisation however is also reinforced and finds refuge in the colonial ecosystem of the neoliberal 'native 'elite'. Seemingly critical perspectives like postcolonial theory/subaltern studies build on an intellectual capital and become ways in which scholar networks find their epistemological grounds in order to succeed in the profession. In this endeavour of the neoliberal academic, performativity operates on another register — that of critical performativity. This includes seemingly anti-colonial frames which do not have principled ethics of their own positionality and theories are deployed simply for intellectual capital and personal gain. Here again this binarisation of praxis and theory produces the effect of emboldening the neoliberal 'native elite'. Under the guise of critical 'theory', neoliberal academics of colour ignore colonial frames they themselves are complicit in and hence their praxis does not become a way to question their theoretical integrity.

The discussion of 'how' as mediating set of principles, guidelines, 'ethics' thus are not just discursive considerations, they must be part of spaces and conditions under which these discussions happen. More importantly, they are ethical questions translated into principles/mediating inter-dialogical frames, an anti-colonial scholar network needs to have so as to not reproduce 'native elitism'. Principles, guidelines or ethical frames can have the ability to guide us, as ways to reclaim our experiences, as conversations of self-reflection, self-growth and as collective and individual healing.

### On 'Not Being Alone' and the Next Phase: Future Collaborations and Communal Engagement

Drawing on my experiences of being connected with Dr. Salt through Dr. Jivraj, I was convinced that we need to counter the 'neo-liberal network' of academia which reinforces 'whiteness' with our own 'principled' ecosystems of support. Through the project, I became more conscious of seeking out other PhDs/staff who were having similar discussions. Not long after our project, the University of Sheffield and University of Sheffield Hallam publicised their informal forums on decolonising research and decolonising methodologies.

If anything, in all of the three instances i.e. white PhD students, discussion with an international Indian scholar activist and at Sheffield University workshop, it became clear to me the importance the mediating principles is these contexts. The idea of grounding principles through which we all can engage with decoloniality are incredibly important to a constructive possibility of a decolonising research. In my experiences in these three instances these were either absent/or partially present. Which in one case lead to uncomfortable, troubling and self-effacing experiences I have faced in other scenarios of 'whiteness' reinforcing itself as the only authority in the room.

### Rethinking Ground Rules? — The Need for a Manifesto for Decolonial Research Ethics

Looking forward, what is paramount in taking the initiative of decolonising research and especially the research collective at University of Kent forward, is to drive home the form, spaces, and dynamics in which conversations around decolonising research are being held. This requires developing, honing and putting into place core principles of the spaces in which we produce knowledge. Dr Salt for example refers to a guiding principles document of the common cause research collective[4] she works with who do research projects with communities. While we think about a more structured, strategic approach to resist within the academic ecosystem, at the most foundational level, we must start with ourselves. Reflecting, re-examining the everyday spaces and dynamics of academic 'work' and build collaborative networks where we can push these subversive ways of resisting in order to further our aim of creating an anti-colonial ecosystem within the colonial university.

### Notes

1  Salt K., 'Keynote Speech', Decolonising the Curriculam Project Conference 2019.  https://www.youtube.com/watch?v=KYglXKq7yJ4&list=PLbAKl g2H-Hdu-v5ZPBMF6hta3PNe-aSob&index=8.

2  Ibid.

3  https://research.kent.ac.uk/sergj/kaleidoscope-network-decolonising-the-university/.

4  https://www.commoncauseresearch.com/, *Common Cause* (2018). Common Cause: Building Research Collaborations between Universities and Black and Minority Ethnic Communities. Bristol University and AHRC Connected Communities Programme.

### References

Ahmad, I. (1978) *Caste and Social Stratification Among Muslims in India.* South Asia Books

Ahmed, S. (2004). Declarations of Whiteness: The Non-Performativity of Anti-Racism. *Borderlands* 3(2), pp. 1–15..

Ambedkar, B.R. (1948). *Untouchables: Who Were They and Why They Became Untouchables.* Amrit Book Company: New Delhi.

Ambedkar, B.R. (2014). *Annihilation of Caste: The Annotated Critical Edition.* New York: Verso Books.

Arday, J. (2017). University and College Union (UCU): Exploring Black and Minority Ethnic (BME) Doctoral Students' Perceptions of a Career in Academia: Experiences, Perceptions and Career Progression. London: Creative Commons, https://www.ucu.org.uk/media/8633/BME-doctoral-students-perceptions-of-an-academic-career/pdf/UCU_Arday_Report_-_June_20171.pdf.

Da Costa, D. and Da Costa, A.E. (2019). Introduction: Cultural Production Under Multiple Colonialisms. *Cultural Studies* 33(3), pp. 343–369.

Dabashi, H. (2015) *Can Non-Europeans Think?* London: Zed Books Ltd.

Fanon, F. (2008) *Black Skin, White Masks.* New York: Grove Press.

Figueira, D.M. (2008). *Otherwise Occupied: Pedagogies of Alterity and the Brahminization of Theory.* New York: Suny Press.

Guru, G. and Sarukkai, S. (2018). *The Cracked Mirror: An Indian Debate on Experience and Theory.* Oxford: Oxford University Press.

Iqbal, M. (1940). *The Secrets of the Self: Asrar-I Khudi.* Forgotten Books.

Jangam, C. (2015). Politics of Identity and the Project of Writing History in Postcolonial India: A Dalit Critique. *Economic and Political Weekly*, 50(40), pp. 63–70.

Joseph-Salisbury, R. (2018). Confronting My Duty as an Academic: We Should All Be Activists. In: Johnson, A., Joseph-Salisbury, R. and Kamunge, B. eds. *The Fire Now: Anti-Racist Scholarship in Times of Explicit Racial Violence.* Zed Books.

Krishnaswamy, R. (2005). Globalization and Its Postcolonial (Dis)Contents: Reading Dalit Writing. *Journal of Postcolonial Writing* 41(1), pp. 69–82.

Mignolo, W.D. (2009). Epistemic Disobedience, Independent Thought and Decolonial Freedom. *Theory, Culture & Society* 26(7–8), pp. 159–181.

Morsi, Y. (2018). The 'Free Speech' of the (Un)Free. *Continuum* 32(4), pp. 474–486.

Naqvi, Z.B., Fletcher, R., Ashiagbor, D., Cruz, K. and Russell, Y. (2019) Back at the Kitchen Table: Reflections on Decolonising and Internationalising With the Global South Socio-Legal Writing Workshops. *Feminist Legal Studies* 22, pp. 123–137.

Patel, S. (2016). Complicating the Tale of 'Two Indians': Mapping 'South Asian' Complicity in White Settler Colonialism Along the Axis of Caste and Anti-Blackness. *Theory & Event* 19(4).

Sevea, I.S. (2012). *The Political Philosophy of Muhammad Iqbal: Islam and Nationalism in Late Colonial India.* Cambridge: Cambridge University Press.

Smith, L.T. (2013). *Decolonizing Methodologies: Research and Indigenous Peoples.* London: Zed Books Ltd.

Tuck, E. and Yang, K.W. (2012). Decolonization Is Not a Metaphor. *Decolonization: Indigeneity, Education & Society* 1(1).

§7

# DECOLONISING THE UNIVERSITY OF KENT: A STRATEGIC RESPONSE

# 19

# Decolonising the University —
# Success, Pitfalls and Next Steps

*Dr Suhraiya Jivraj*
*University of Kent*

Education is an important element in the struggle for human rights. It is the means to help our children and our people rediscover their identity, and thereby increase their self-respect. *Education is our passport to the future, for tomorrow belongs only to the people who prepare for it today.*

(Malcolm X 1964. Emphasis added)

## Welcoming Students (and Staff) of Colour to the Academy

These words of Black radical Muslim civil rights campaigner Malcolm X, delivered at the Organization of Afro-American Unity (OAAU) founding forum in 1964, were used by one of the few Black women professors in the UK to welcome nearly six hundred students to Kent Law School in September 2019. These powerful words set the tone for an inclusive law school for all students and staff to participate in and actively build a culture of belonging in our shared learning and scholarly community. The law school is well known amongst other UK law schools and internationally, as having a distinctive *critical* approach, placing *law* within the wider context of society. Its diverse and international approach bucks the trend in research which demonstrates how national higher education institutions (HEIs) remain literal 'ivory' towers (Tate and Grabriel 2018; Rollock 2019). Almost twenty years ago I found my place within the academy also thanks to the act of being welcomed and given space to be, explore and develop my authentic self in all its complex facets. This is no easy feat with increasing data highlighting structural barriers still existing despite Equalities legislation and policy, making it extremely difficult for people of colour to enter, progress and have their work recognised equally within HEIs (Bhopal 2018; Gabriel & Tate 2018; Rollock 2019).[1] I remain here, within an HEI, not least because the words of Malcom X and the ethos they embody continue to welcome me back each year. They remind me that I am entitled to inhabit this space; indeed, that I must in order continue to do the everyday work of my teachers and those before them who have empowered students to think critically and realise their potential. This labour is an essential part of the process of 'dropping ladders' around oneself for the next generation, to ensure the pipeline of undergraduate students to postgraduate and academics of the future remains flowing and unblocked in both quiet, 'unseen' and explicit ways.

There is an abundance of transformative pedagogy, from Paulo Freire (1996) to bell hooks (1994) available to help us as educators to respond to increasing student calls for change. We must draw on this work to respond to students demanding a 'liberated curriculum' or classes that decolonise our minds and thinking, to question authority and epistemic violence of monoliths such as Cecil Rhodes in Oxford or Keynes in Kent. These voices are being amplified across the country through occupy movements at Goldsmiths and Warwick, through student unions campaigning against eugenics conferences at UCL, or at SOAS and not least at my own University where the SU ran its 'Diversify My Curriculum' in 2017/18. To add to this list there is now Decolonise University of Kent (Decolonise UoK), with its manifesto of recommendations based on empirical research; 'Stripping the White Walls' podcast speaking to both students about their life on campus, and academics that they take inspiration from. As part of the Decolonise University of Kent movement, Ahmed Memon developed a postgraduate research collective with the other students. This has formed a vibrant and talented committee engaging in outreach and community building with other decolonising student groups (such as QMUL, Keele, Lancaseter) with whom they have been developing a creative portfolio of work. Some of this body of work will be featured at the Decolonise University of Kent event 2020, which will be headlined by activist, educator, rapper and mentor, Lowkey.

## Alarm Bells in a Departmental Meeting

This amazingly accomplished project all run by students — facilitated by me with a handful of colleagues grew from what I had intended to be a modest experiment in teaching in a final year optional module that I convene: Race, Religion and Law. The thinking process began three years ago when I had been sitting in an unremarkable departmental meeting until my gentle ruminations became interrupted by 'race' alarm bells. A central university presentation was being delivered that highlighted 'black and Asian' students as having 'attainment gaps' followed by a haze of graphs and stats. Instinctive discomfort rose within me as my racism radar picked up on what seemed to me as crass racial stereotyping about the behaviours and achievements of 'Indian students' vs 'black students' vs 'East Asian' students. My misgivings about this 'data' were not diminished by 'explanations' of the need for this 'equalities' work because the problem — disparities in achievement of degree grades — sounded too much like it lay at the door of the students and not the institutions, and that did not speak to my experience as a former student nor to those now thousands of students I have taught over the last two decades. However, I needed to put my hypothesis — that the problem was constructed in a way that reinforced racialisation rather than challenged it, to the test. Did the students know that those of them labelled 'BME'[2] or 'BAME'[3] had been saddled with yet another categorisation — that old colonial habit used to understand its 'other' — this time as under-achievers or statistical attainment gaps? If so, how did they feel about it? Were their experiences in the classroom and on campus impacting their learning experiences and outcomes? I was curious and needed to know but not just anecdotally in my role as their Teacher, Academic Advisor or even as a Chief Examiner, nor even in the form of general student feedback. I needed to understand this as 'data' through a fully approved qualitative research process that I knew the students would have to undertake themselves, albeit under my supervisory guidance. Having taught my optional module for a number of years and knowing that it was popular and transformative, particularly for students of colour, I knew they would be up for the task. They were constantly feeding back that they relished the opportunity both in workshops and through their assessment to explore both historical and contemporary issues that enable them to acquire 'consciousness of their own position and struggle' in society and education. One student stated:

> This stuff is so important, why don't we know about it, why didn't we learn about it in school? We are not taught about how Britain's treatment of black people has basically been justified by and through the law. It is shocking!

After 'the conversation with Dave' (see the Introduction) I designed a plan to embed a research project within the module which would also form part of the assessment. In Spring 2018 I applied for a for a teaching enhancement (TESSA) award which was successful.

The project, originally entitled 'BAME students as change actors and co-producers of knowledge: towards an inclusive curriculum' aimed to empower BAME students to develop academic 'capital' (to use the EDI industry language) and become co-producers of knowledge and stronger stakeholders in their own education within the law school. The project sought to achieve this by facilitating the students to research (through running focus groups) to voice and share with other students their experiences around race, racialisation and (un)belonging on campus, in the classroom and through the curriculum in safe 'café' style spaces. This research would then be disseminated as their collective findings through publication in various formats and a half day workshop.

The project was launched by Dr Jason Arday — on World Mental Health Day (10 October 2018) — who gave the keynote to a packed lecture theatre of students who were captivated by his research on black mental health within higher education. It was like suddenly we had been given permission in a safe space to talk about the specific mental health issues and challenges that students of colour face. As Jason stated on the day many students would not even be able to talk about this topic with their parents or friends because of what they would have gone through as a result of racialisation and racism in their lives. Many students' families would have been of the Windrush generation and or been migrants having to leave homes for extremely complex socio-economic reasons. He acknowledged that the appropriate counsellors and support were rarely available in our institutions and this was certainly confirmed in the manifesto research findings. After that event many more students from beyond the law school wanted to get involved so I applied for a second TESSA grant to ensure that more students could have the opportunity to be involved.

The students then set up a committee, a regular reading group and from there the Decolonising the Curriculum Project, *as they named it,* was born. Students who were in their third year were then invited to submit applications to become focus group leaders and form a team of paid researchers to begin the process of co-producing knowledge and becoming leaders in their own educational journeys.

## Collaborating With Students

Going through the research process including the ethics approval format — from a student perspective — was also crucial for me in reflecting on the variety of factors that affect the student experience at university, of which academics are often unaware. For example, the impact of the government's Prevent strategy on Muslim students' visceral fear of surveillance on campus and the barriers this creates in accessing services; experiences of gendered racism faced by black women, and the additional barriers in obtaining culturally sensitive and appropriate student support including counselling if you are a disabled and/or from a non-English background. Through discussions in the training sessions we collectively decided on the themes of the focus groups, developed a set of questions, identified the venues that would be most appropriate, safe and comfortable and other tangible and intangible factors that would enable the participants to be able to freely express their experiences in class and on campus. The students managed to engaged more than 100 other students from across the university into three distinct but overlapping areas which constitute the framework for the manifesto as a qualitative piece of research.

The manifesto was then launched in March 2019 to an audience of two hundred people.[4] Attendees feedback (including from staff at various HEIs) overwhelmingly reported how much they had learnt and benefitted from the power in the room that was created by bringing both students and eminent academics of colour (Karen Salt, Deborah Gabriel, Jason Arday, Francesca Sobande, Azeezat Johnson, Remi Joseph-Salisbury, Lez Henry and the Building the Anti-Racist Classroom Collective) together to explore the themes of the manifesto including tackling racism in the curriculum, on campus, and in classrooms as a key barrier to belonging and attainment.

The project's ethos of collaborating with students as experts in their own experiences of the learning community was rewarded beyond proper remuneration, employability points, or other forms of recognition with the opportunities to develop skills and confidence with academics in whom they saw themselves reflected. As one focus group leader student stated:

> Coming to class, the reading groups and meetings was not a chore, it was a pleasure, we got to know one another and really be able to exchange ideas and support each other. It was hard and scary at times, the responsibility of running the focus groups and writing up the difficult and sensitive things other students had talked about. But I also loved doing it, grew more confident as we were writing and presenting it at the conference. I didn't think I could publish work let alone co-author a book. (Third year law student)

This is a very different way to engage with students which allows them to see themselves as stakeholders in their own education rather than being represented as quantitative data — 'BME attainment gap' statistics — in University diversity reports which does not capture the nuance and complexity of their lived realities. Empowerment for self-determination at the grassroots level is key as is apparent from student-led movements that have already effected change in the curriculum and HE globally.

**Where Now? Next Steps**

The Decolonise the Curriculum Project 2018/19 has now officially ended, having successfully achieved its aiming of producing the manifesto. It also appeared as a case study in the recently published UUK and NUS report Closing the Gap (2019) on 'BME achievement' in HE and featured one of the stage three (finalist) project students Joy Olugboyega (who I have taught since stage one as a Certificate in Law student at our Medway Campus on a Widening Participation path) on the front page.[5] The students also provided footage for the UUK promotional materials and presented the manifesto to Baroness Amos (co-author of the report) at its launch conference at SOAS in May 2019. We also attended an event hosted by the former Speaker of the House of Commons, Mr John Bercow MP, who was delighted to be presented with the manifesto.[6] Clearly this work is garnering interest and already having a significant impact beyond the university. The students have won awards for their contribution to Diversity and Inclusion and we have had many enquiries from student groups and academics from other universities, eager to find out more about the work we have done. Both Dave and I as well as the students have provided talks and trainings in a range of departments across the country and abroad including within our own university.

My 'next steps' document compiled for the university's executive group outlined how key student concerns — particularly experiences of racism — as articulated in the manifesto could be addressed in three key areas:

Pedagogy and powerful learning experiences: The colour of our curriculum

Race, identity & belonging: Promoting Inclusion / Countering Exclusion

Student voice & co-production with academics: Stakeholders within the university

As with the manifesto the 'next steps' document specifically responded to the institutionally funded University of Kent Student Success (EDI) Project Phase II strategy which acknowledges the need to affirm that the 'white curriculum acts as a barrier to inclusivity' because 'it fails to legitimise contributions to knowledge from people of colour'. It also states — under the heading 'Race, Identity & Belonging' that

> we will ensure that our staff body remains diverse, so that our curriculum reflects and addresses a range of perspectives. How can this be operationalised?

It is interesting that this heading ends with a question being posed demonstrating the gap in knowledge and implementation at institutional level. In a sense, the time seemed right to lobby and be hopeful for joined up institutional structural change, that goes beyond reading lists and also tackles racism and other forms of exclusion directly as part of the University's education and EDI strategy. After all, there was clear willingness on the part of leadership to listen and engage with the project having been supported by the Race Equality Champion (Deputy Vice Chancellor) and the Education Deputy Vice Chancellor who stated after the 2019 manifesto launch conference:

> This excellent event demonstrates that the University is committed to providing an inclusive and diverse environment for all its students and staff. We know we have more to do to deliver this — we welcome our students' views and contributions and look forward to discussing next steps.[7]

However, as leading academic and campaigner in the area of education and social justice, Professor Kalwant Bhopal (2018) reminds us: UK

HE is 'one of those occupied spaces where rhetoric does not translate to outcome' despite commitment to the ideals of valuing 'diversity' and 'internationalisation' in HE contexts. The question remains then: what has really changed at the institutional level particularly in relation to implementing the recommendations in the manifesto?

## Institutional Change

What has been achieved in the three areas that recommendations were made? What have been the successes in terms of implementation in the three areas?

*1. Pedagogy and Powerful Learning Experiences: The Colour of Our Curriculum*

As a recent UCL Institute of Education Study shows university reading lists are far from representative of the student populations within their programmes. Rather, reading lists tend to be dominated by white, male, Eurocentric knowledge. (Schuchan Bird & Pitman 2019). This is corroborated in the Decolonise University of Kent student findings which calls for more work by scholars of colour, including from the global south so that the curriculum reflects and addresses a range of experiences whilst also promoting cultural democracy. As stated in the manifesto, this is also crucial to 'develop *all* students into critical and analytical thinkers *and* leaders within their education'. This work had already begun as part of the project through the Decolonise Research Collective set up by Ahmed Memon. He consulted postgraduate students through both the Graduate school and the law school to audit the library resources specifically geared towards the needs of postgraduate research and in particular from the global south. He then worked with the library staff and under my leadership to ensure that the resources they needed were available by the end of the year.

In relation to undergraduates, Dave — in his capacity as a Student Success Project Manager — had already developed the idea of a reading list review project in 2015 when he realised that a number of subjects at the University only used European thinkers and had virtually no non-European scholarship. Although the thought of 'decolonising' reading lists at that point seemed rather radical in the Garden of England location of Kent, there was awareness that reading list audits were happening elsewhere. The project was then piloted with Dr Barbara Adewumi in the department of Sociology, Social Policy and Social Research working with two students Evangeline Ageyman and Collins Kudo-Mensah who audited fifteen modules, did the data analysis (see chapter 16) and have subsequently spoken eloquently about the consciousness raising impact that doing this work has had on them individually as well the contribution they have made to kickstarting a movement. This project is remarkable — and in my view — radical, for being an all-Black staff and student collaboration. The work of auditing reading lists has now been scaled up by the university through channels like the library and putting in place a 'Diversity Mark' scheme. This is a success of sorts, in that awareness about lack of diversity in reading lists has certainly been raised. However, the way it does so is problematic in two ways. Firstly, it marks out — and possibly hyper-visibilises — literature by scholars of colour and from the global south as 'different'. Difference in this context is predicated on racialisation perpetuated by a legacy of colonial classificatory regimes (Jivraj 2020). Secondly, and this is what so often happens, is that paradox of hyper-visibilisation can also bring with it erasure. As Dave S.P. Thomas notes,

> the reading list review project has been morphed into a Diversity Mark project in some schools and a department at the university of Kent. While the Reading List Review project is undergirded by a critical race theory methodology with clear considerations for schools and departments who are motivated to review their reading lists, a clear methodology and support for the #Decolonising project is not evident in the Diversity Mark approach. (Thomas 2020)[8]

The radical potential of a team of Black staff and students is no where to be seen in the poised photographs of the University library staff winning the Times Higher Education Award in the Outstanding Library Team category partly for 'innovation in fostering co-created reading lists' (Havergal 2019). In this sense success can also be simultaneously a pitfall and an act of rendering the visceral labour that comes from a legacy of overcoming racism in the first place, disappeared. Nonetheless, within the project itself, this only serves as a reminder of the ever looming dangers of co-optation, for we still are lodgers in the Masters House and that much time and effort will need to be sustained to change and embed a new culture of reading. Thomas (2020) asks the important question:

Following the initial Decolonise UKC conference where students also challenged the university to broaden the perspectives presented within their curricula is it somewhat myopic to believe that institutional success has been achieved?

### 2. Race, Identity & Belonging: Promoting Inclusion / Countering Exclusion

As the Equalities and Human Rights Commission report (2019) on 'Tackling Racial Harassment: Universities Challenged' (2019) highlights racism on campus is a significant factor in both students and staff of colour feeling alienated within HE. A key barrier to addressing this is that both feel unable to report incidents of racism either through a lack of knowledge of how to do so, or a lack of faith that any positive action would actually be taken. It is unsurprising then that training or small measures to align wellbeing & student support with the diverse student population will have little effect in making inroads into the lack of trust and sense of belonging. Rather, it has been crucial to find ways to engage staff to be culturally sensitive so that students can feel that they are able to access services rather than get caught up in a 'circle of fear' with little trust that they will receive the help they may need. The student's own suggestion has been to set up what they named *Kaleidoscope Hub*, coined by Lisa Shoko and Ahmed Memon, as a principled community space where students of colour would feel able to access and develop strong networks of support and sense of belonging and find help to deal with racialisation and racism on campus (see chapter 17). To work towards a physical hub which had informally been housed in the common room of the Kent Law School research Centre for Sexuality, Race & Gender Justice (SeRGJ)[9] of which I have been co-director, we set up the Kaleidoscope Network[10] of staff and students of colour and allies. We hoped that this network, in conjunction with the newly formed BAME/staff of colour network, would be a vehicle to drive forward implementation of the manifesto recommendations including eventually having a more central Kaleidoscope Hub space.

In relation to the Kaleidoscope Network, the student and staff members worked together to draft principles that members would need to pledge to, a white allies survival guide and reading list to facilitate collaboration rather than co-optation or situations of 'white fragility' (Di'Angelo 2018). So far the Kaleidoscope Network has primarily focused on working with the Student Services EDI officer, who has actively worked with students gaining input for example on the university's harassment reporting mechanism (https://ink.kent.ac.uk/).

As she states:

> The conversations started by the Decolonise the Curriculum Project and, later, the Kaleidoscope Network, have started to trigger a shift in this way of thinking and working. They provide a framework for difficult conversations to be had and for Kent to shine a spotlight on itself and identify exactly what and where the issues are. Decolonise in particular has provided multiple platforms for BAME voices to be heard, both in terms of talking about their own experiences within the Higher Education Sector and provided opportunities to hear from others via their speaker programmes. The fact that this work represents grass root action is particularly powerful, and they have won awards in recognition of this. They are not afraid to tackle the difficult conversations that often push the University past its pain threshold and have ensured that race and racism will remain at the top of the EDI agenda for the foreseeable future. The new InK reporting tool (launched in September 2019 and originally set up for reporting incidents of sexual abuse and rape) has since been adapted to allow for the reporting of racism and other forms of discrimination and harassment, and work is currently being undertaken off the back of this to increase the cultural competency of our student support services to ensure that support for students is appropriate and effective. Conversations are now taking place which are looking at ways of truly mapping and identifying the scale of racism at Kent in a manner that will allow for positive change to take place via projects to capture the student and staff voice, and encourage a greater reporting of incidents of racism. This represents the start of a seismic cultural shift in thinking, and one that, whilst slow moving, has the potential to truly create a University culture that is open, welcoming and feels like it belongs to all.

*3. Student Voice & Co-Production With Academics: Stakeholders Within the University*

In a post-Brexit, hostile environment climate where Muslim students also feel hyper-surveilled as a result of the Government's Prevent Duty there is much still to do but it is clear from what is stated above that the 'seismic shift' that needs to take place has began in some corners at least. Of course, this needs to happen at senior leadership level as well where the student voice and staff-student collaboration must take place beyond working with student union sabbatical officers. There are some who are leading the way as is evident here:

As a Master of one of the University of Kent's colleges I am responsible for looking after the welfare and the conduct of over 3000 students. In this role, instances of racist behaviour and action towards and by students of the college should be reported to me. While we will investigate all such reports and action will be taken against the perpetrators, I have become increasingly conscious that students of colour too often choose not to report such behaviours. The work of the Decolonise the Curriculum Project, the manifesto produced by the students and the various events organised have been extremely important to me in starting to explore why this may be the case. The creation of the Kaleidoscope Network has been a first step in trying to find collective solutions.

This statement demonstrates the amazing potential and results that could be actualised within HE if only we could understand how to collaborate with students as experts, leaders and co-producers of knowledge through initiatives like the kaleidoscope network. The UUK/ NUS #Closing the Gap report (2019) in which the DecoloniseUKC project was featured makes five recommendations including the need for universities to have conversations about race. I would also add to that explicitly that those conversations need to be about racism. My experience as an academic lead for a student decolonising the curriculum project is that we are far away from that moment. As many critical race and decolonial studies scholars have argued the higher education sector in the global north is far too embroiled in the colonial logics that underpin racial capitalism and white innocence (Wekker 2016). No wonder we still have a long way to go before sufficient processes are in place to ensure transparent *accountability* from university leadership to students and staff for all forms of racism whether structural, institutional or as micro-aggressions. However, empowering students is still very much necessary so we must find ways to keep facilitating students to articulate their stories. We have certainly been fortunate to work and collaborate with so many creative people of colour who have helped us to find creative means whether art, spoken word, music and podcasts. Through the Kaleidoscope Hub activities and decolonial café at Queen Mary University, working with other decolonising student groups and the Building the Anti-racist Classroom Collective students and staff are collectively unleashing depths of story-telling about life at university and beyond. This will be our focus at the next Decolonise University of `Kent event on stories of (un)belonging with rapper, activist and educator Lowkey.

**Notes**

1  See also: latest (2018–19) Higher Education Statistics Agency (Hesa) data https://www.hesa.ac.uk/news/23-01-2020/sb256-higher-education-staff-statistics that demonstrates the number of Black, Asian and ethnic minority staff being promoted and recruited, particularly to senior (leadership) roles has fallen in the last academic year. Chris Skidmore, higher education minister for England, has criticised universities for failing to tackle the inequalities resulting in this fall describing it as 'unacceptable'. https://www.theguardian.com/education/2020/jan/23/minister-criticises-lack-of-senior-black-uk-academics; https://www.thetimes.co.uk/article/no-top-jobs-for-black-academics-in-britain-s-universities-73l2pbnt7;  https://www.telegraph.co.uk/news/2020/01/23/number-black-academics-top-university-roles-officially-zero/.

2  Black and minority ethnic.

3  Black, Asian and minority ethnic.

4  https://decoloniseukc.org/2019/07/25/decoloniseukc-conference-footage/.

5  https://www.universitiesuk.ac.uk/policy-and-analysis/reports/Pages/bame-student-attainment-uk-universities-closing-the-gap.aspx.

6  https://blogs.kent.ac.uk/law-news/2019/06/13/decolonising-the-curriculum-project-manifesto-presented-to-speaker-of-the-house-of-commons/.

7  https://www.kent.ac.uk/news/kentlife/21678/kent-students-launch-decoloniseukc-manifesto.

8  https://www.advance-he.ac.uk/news-and-views/Democracy-Diversity-and-Decolonisation.

9  http://research.kent.ac.uk/sergj.

10  https://research.kent.ac.uk/sergj/kaleidoscope-network-decolonising-the-university/.

**References**

Bhopal, K., & Pitkin, C. (2020). 'Same Old Story, Just a Different Policy': Race and Policy Making in Higher Education in the UK. *Race Ethnicity and Education.*

Diangelo, R. (2018). *White Fragility: Why Is It so Hard for White People to Talk about Racism.* London: Allen Lane an Imprint of Penguin Books.

Freire, P. (1996). *Pedagogy of the Oppressed.* London: Penguin.

Gabriel, D. and Tate, S.A (2017). *Inside the Ivory Tower: Narratives of Women of Colour Surviving and Thriving in British Academia.* London: Trentham Books.

Havergal, C. (2019). Times Higher Education Awards 2019: Winners Announced. THE World University Rankings [Online]. Available at: https://www.

timeshighereducation.com/news/times-higher-education-awards-2019-winners-announced.

hooks, b. (1994). *Teaching to Transgress. Education as the Practice of Freedom.* London: Routledge.

Jivraj, S. (2020). Between a Rock and a Hard Place. *Interventions: Journal of Postcolonial Studies* 22(4). https://doi.org/10.1080/1369801X.2020.1753559.

Melamed, J. (Spring 2015). Racial Capitalism. *Critical Ethnic Studies* 1(1), pp. 76–85.

Rollock, N. (2019). Staying Power. The Career Experiences and Strategies of UK Black Female Professors. UCU Report. https://www.ucu.org.uk/media/10075/Staying-Power/pdf/UCU_Rollock_February_2019.pdf.

Schucan Bird, K., & Pitman, L. (2019). How Diverse Is Your Reading List? Exploring Issues of Representation and Decolonisation in the UK. *Higher Education.*

Thomas, D. (2020). Democracy, Diversity and Decolonisation: Staff-Student Partnerships in a Reading List Review [Online]. Available at: https://www.advance-he.ac.uk/news-and-views/Democracy-Diversity-and-Decolonisation.

UUK/NUS (2019). Black, Asian And Minority Ethnic Student Attainment at UK Universities: #Closingthegap. https://www.universitiesuk.ac.uk/policy-and-analysis/reports/Documents/2019/bame-student-attainment-uk-universities-closing-the-gap.pdf.

Wekker, G. (2016). *White Innocence.* Duke University Press.

X, Malcolm. (June 28, 1964). Speech at the Organization of Afro-American Unity (OAAU) Founding Forum. Audubon Ballroom.

§8

# POWER TO THE PEOPLE

20

# Letter to the 1%

*Lowkey*

Talking in terms of power. Where the power is, who's shaping the condition of our lives, who determines the quality of the air we breathe, the food we eat, the water we drink, the kinda jobs we can have, the images we have to deal with and such.

(Michael Parenti)

If I can sing this song without you maybe all is well
If we can sing this song without you we don't need your wealth
*This is my letter to the 1%*
If I can sing this song without you maybe all is well
If we can sing this song without you we don't need your wealth

Power to those who read bell hooks, power to those who sell books
Power to those who know how the inside of a cell looks
All those feeling helpless, forgotten and discarded
Power to the strange fruit you thought was rotten in the garden
Power to those sitting alone, seeking solace in the calmness
Power to those feeling stained, know your tomorrow isn't tarnished
Power to those that sweep the streets with more knowledge than PhD's
Power to those that keep their keys, return this promise, please believe
Power to those that suffer in silence, those it hurts to hear
Power to those that hold their ground, power to those that persevere
Power to those that love humanity more than they love style
Power to immigrants probably raising Donald Trump's child
Power to the blind who can't imagine what sight is
Those staring at the moon and all those working night-shifts
Power to the readers, the writers, the illiterate
Power to those that struggle to decolonise their syllabus
Power to the shy ones, always struggle to make friends
And the half of humanity worth less than eight men
Power to those that risked their life to dig the coltan from the ground

For the mic I'm spitting on and the phone you're holding now
Power to those that build the stadium they're playing in
Power to those that mowed the grass and stitched the ball that they're playing
with
Power to every rapper that doesn't rap about killing
Power to the builders who built buildings that outlived them

If I can sing this song without you maybe all is well
If we can sing this song without you we don't need your wealth[1]

---

1  An excerpt from the original song entitled 'Letter to the 1%'. Included with
permission from the author.

# Conclusions

Dr Jason Arday
University of Durham

All for One ... One for All ... If we all join hands, we shall not fall.

Racism in higher education impacts many Black, Asian and Minority Ethnic (BAME) staff and students in a way that is truly impossible to fathom, such is the perniciousness of this discriminatory instrument. Racism within the academy occupies a centrality that straddles upon Whiteness. Anti-racist movements have a long and persistent history of tackling inequality in the hope of creating truly egalitarian spaces within our society. The academy remains a microcosm of that society and as such the importance of a space that is reflective of an ever-increasing diverse multi-cultural society is paramount. My understanding of higher education sector very much oscillates between frustration and hope. This hope is reflected in many student and scholar-activist led movements such as *Why is My Curriculum White, Rhodes Must Fall and Why isn't my Professor Black?*

This hope has further been strengthened by new anti-racist movements and observing the baton being taken up by a new generation of student scholar-activists. I was extremely fortunate to be a part of a launch that would become the latest contribution towards dismantling racism in higher education: Decolonising the Curriculum Project — Through the Kaleidoscope at the University of Kent also known as Decolonise UKC (and later Decolonise UoK). On the 10 March 2019 on World Mental Health Day, the collective would discuss the impact of racism particularly in higher education on mental health and wellness. I was able to offer some insights based on research findings regarding BAME mental health in academy and this proved to be a catalyst for others to be able to safely disseminate their experiences of racism and altered mental state, whilst highlighting the lack of culturally appropriate, psychological and pastoral interventions available to them.

The issues addressed by the collective were framed by a manifesto which was focused on not only addressing patterns of racism at the University of Kent but also the sector more generally. The focus on themes associated with diversity of perspectives was particularly pertinent because the absence of scholars of colour was regarded as a central tenet towards improving 'the colour of the curriculum'. This was particularly pertinent because of the growing need to have a curriculum that reflects and addresses a wider range of experiences in promoting cultural democracy. The sense of community developed within this *collective* has reverberated throughout the sector as communities of students of colour throughout the United Kingdom (UK) begin to find solace in the power of unilateral networks which have unified students, professional staff and academics.

The idea of co-production has been a powerful tenet of the Decolonise UoK collective, it has ensured that within this movement the student voice occupies the centre ground. Part of this voice has strongly advocated for developing pipelines for students of colour wanting to pursue an academic career with considerations given towards the lack of fully funded studentship for BAME students throughout the sector as highlighted in the recent Leading Routes report; *The Broken Pipeline Report: Barriers to Black PhD Students Accessing Research Council Funding* by Paulette Williams, Sukhi Bathm, Dr Jason Arday and Chantelle Lewis (September 2019).

Observing the students that were part of this collective was truly inspiring. To witness such incredibly gifted young BAME individuals mobilising change within their institution aided by the talismanic trio of Dr Suhraiya Jivraj, Dave S.P. Thomas and Sheree Palmer was a reminder to us all of the cohesive endeavour required to decolonise the academy. This would leave an indelible imprint on the audience fortunate to present on that day and myself. There was a feeling that these students were paying substantial sums of money to study and leave with a degree, the guilt that then ensues relates to the perhaps idealistic notion that these students should not be having to relieve themselves and the institution of the unwanted burden of racism. Similarly, as someone observing this and the impact that this cohort of students continue to have throughout the sector, it is quite remarkable that this collective have achieved a feat that is truly hard to quantify, but perhaps the easier way to measure this impact is to see the gradual changes now ensuing at the University of Kent with regards to decolonising the curriculum which now involves students' having more autonomy and agency in the curriculum design process.

The internal reach of the Decolonise UoK manifesto in March 2019, has helped to inform a strategy document that currently signposts the University of Kent's Executive Group, regarding how key points from the manifesto can be implemented in attempting to create greater diversification in all aspects of the university particularly with regards to aspects of belonging, attainment, curriculum and academic progression. In developing this academic capital BAME students have become change agents, co-producers of knowledge and stakeholders within their own educational journeys in higher education. The potency of this intervention lies in the fact that this is a student-led project which enables a capturing of nuanced and complex lived reality of their racialised experiences.

The work of Jivraj, Thomas and Palmer has been equally as remarkable. The vanity and ego-driven nature of the academy, rarely creates situations of reciprocity where academics and students become equal partners in activism and knowledge construction. The efforts of these three individuals in removing power dynamics and hierarchies is not to be under-estimated and is to be applauded. Their efforts were poignantly captured during a question and answer session during the launch where a panellist asked: what can we do to support Decolonise UoK ... to which a member of the collective responded 'just be our Suhraiya, Dave and Sheree'. This comment for me really immortalised the efforts of these three individuals. They stand as equally remarkable as the students they are actively mobilising.

Within the sector we recognise racism to be a sophisticated instrument that is weaponised to debilitating and sustained effect at the expense of BAME students and staff. Interventions like this re-centre the chorus of hope and provide a stimulus for cultivating not only institutional change but sector-wide change. The Decolonise UoK collective reminds us all that it is our collective endeavour that will ultimately dismantle racism. The truth of this stems from a very succinct, yet powerful anecdote ... there is always power in the collective.

We as a sector and custodians of the academy are eternally grateful to the selfless endeavour of the Decolonise UoK collective in attempting to create an inclusive academy that is reflective of our multi-cultural and diverse society.

# Afterword

*Professor Emeritus Heidi Safia Mirza*
*Goldsmiths University*

It was a chilly October evening in the autumn of 2019 when I visited University of Kent at Canterbury to deliver the inaugural keynote to the launch of both the newly established BAME staff network and Decolonise UoK Kaleidoscope Network — but what a warm and overwhelming welcome I received! I was struck by the energy and enthusiasm of BAME staff and students and their earnest commitment to decolonise the curriculum and affect the antiracist politics of their institution. We sat huddled around cups of hot tea in the buzzing Kaleidoscope Hub in the Centre for Sexuality, Race and Gender Justice (SeRGJ) surrounded by radical books by Franz Fanon, Angela Davis, Malcolm X, Steve Biko, and inspirational posters of Frida Kahlo, Che Guevara, and Marcus Garvey — among many other of my heroes! It reminded me of my student days in 1970s, when we believed everything was possible and as Sam Cook's Civil Rights song reassured us .... 'A change is gonna come!'

Like these students at Kent, I too was involved in the student movement in the University of East Anglia over 40 years ago! We campaigned to free Palestine, dismantle Apartheid in South Africa and bring down the racist regime of Rhodesia — I still remember the freedom bell ringing out across the campus at midnight in 1979 to herald in the New Zimbabwe, and the euphoria of partying till the early morning.

Now, as a Professor in the establishment, I am still passionate about decolonising movements and their revolutionary intellectual project to decentre the dominance of the Western canon of European thought which lies at the heart of our 'hidden curriculum'. Grassroots student movements like Decolonise UoK and its Kaleidoscope Network are rooted in the long arc of history for the struggle for racial justice that reaches back 100 years to the early twentieth century, when Black and Asian anti-colonial and liberation scholars in India, Africa and the Caribbean began their intellectual struggle for freedom and independence from British imperial rule.

Now, in this particular Millennial moment, at the confluence of neoliberal economics, post-race politics, and new technology, the spark of decolonial student activism is being re-ignited. The mantra of this twenty-first century radical decolonial movement that, *the university is not racist — the university is racism*' alludes to the fact that the very structures and systems that constitute the white Western academy are still designed to reproduce institutions that benefits the interests of the white privileged elite. What is clear now, however, is that this decolonising movement represents a 'tipping point', marking a fundamental shift in global power relations, in which the old colonial and white settler regimes of the fading metropole — characterised by class elitism and white supremacy, are being challenged by the 'irresistible' demands of a new tech savvy multicultural generation of disenfranchised BAME and diasporic international students from the global South. Though intellectual and activist endeavour Black, Asian and global majority scholars of colour now campaign for honest, open 'decolonial dialogues' with their institutions that offer the possibility of a new inclusive geopolitics of knowledge that challenges the dominance of the academy's 'hidden white curriculum'. The landmark Decolonise UKC Manifesto and its later work through the Kaleidoscope Network represents a global postcolonial 'thought revolution' that aims to unsettle and reconstitute taken for granted systems of Eurocentric knowledge production upon which the Western academy is built.

One of the key tactics of the wider global decolonial student movement has been to displace or rename the material manifestation of the imperial and colonial legacies embodied in the statues and buildings on the campuses and beyond that celebrate and, as such, expose the violence of the racist imperial project. The *RhodesMustFall* de-colonial student movement in South Africa in 2015 successfully brought down the statue of the racist British colonialist Cecil Rhodes and triggered a new wave of global decolonial student activism in America and UK. The spontaneous power of this movement spread like a flame to the Metropole of Oxford, Cambridge and London where students also rose up with campaigns such as 'Why is My Curriculum White?', 'Why isn't My Professor Black', #ITooAmOxford and #RhodesMustFall Oxford (RMFO) movement. In this vein the students of Decolonise UKC have challenged the naming of the John Maynard Keyes building and called for an end to inappropriate pedagogy and outdated ethnocentric curriculum practices in their landmark Kaleidoscope Conference and Manifesto.

However, there is a new unprecedented dimension facing the radical student's movement now. In the technological age of social media, we are witnessing virulent and hostile exchanges that characterise the White establishment's backlash against students of colour who dare to challenge the dominant white narrative of the centrality of European modernity. The battle ground for a more open political and culturally representative curriculum and 'safe spaces' to work this out are ridiculed as 'politically correct', a fundamental threat to liberal democracy, and an affront to the sanctity of (white) 'freedom and speech.'

More than ever we need allies. Institutional racism is still endemic in our universities and 50 years of equality and diversity policies have failed to 'dismantle the masters house'. At the launch of the BAME staff and Kaleidoscope Network, I was struck by the deep emotional and intellectual investment of the BAME staff, led by Dave S.P. Thomas and Suhraiya Jivraj, who as 'outsiders within' are essential to finding resources and driving the project to decolonise from within the university. Dedicated Decolonise UoK students such as Anamika Misra and Ahmed Memon gave up precious study time to interview me for their student podcast series 'Stripping the White Walls' where I learnt of the vigil on campus to support their Muslim brothers and sisters, the campaigns for LGBTQ rights, and the unacceptable scandal of the black student attainment gap. In the end, it is our everyday acts of resistance through intellectual generosity, love and kindness that makes a difference. Viva the revolution students and staff of University of Kent at Canterbury!! You are leading the way to a brighter better future for your comrades.